To Chancellor Kim Wilcox,

An important event in Riverside's history.

Arthur L. Littleworth

NO EASY WAY

Integrating Riverside Schools − A Victory for Community

A Personal Reflection
Arthur L. Littleworth, Esq.

Library of Congress Control Number: 2014950086
Trade Paperback: ISBN 978-0-9839575-5-3
Hard Cover: ISBN 978-0-9839575-7-7

Manufactured in the United States
Book design by Geographics

Cover photo: Vintage postcard of Riverside, California, ca. 1960, courtesy of Steve Lech, author of *Riverside in Vintage Postcards*.

Contemporary photographs in *No Easy Way* contributed by Douglas McCulloh.

Douglas McCulloh is a photographer, writer, and curator. His exhibition record includes Victoria and Albert Museum, London; Central Academy of Fine Arts, Beijing; Smithsonian Institution, Washington D.C.; Musée de l'Elysee, Lausanne; Musée Nicéphore Niépce, France; and Centro de la Imagen, Mexico City. McCulloh's fifth book, *The Great Picture: Making the World's Largest Photograph* (with The Legacy Project collaborative) was published in 2011 by Hudson Hills Press, New York. He is a four-time recipient of project support from the California Council for the Humanities and has curated fourteen exhibitions, including three for the California Museum of Photography. His latest curatorial project focuses on international blind photographers and has traveled to museums in Moscow, Mexico City, Seoul, Denver, Florida, and Washington D.C. among other locations.

The old order changeth, yielding place to new. . .
Tennyson, Morte d'Arthur (1842)

This memoir is dedicated to all who helped make integration in
Riverside a success: the determined parents who wanted an equal
education for their children; the Board of Education and the educators
who worked tirelessly to facilitate a resolution that would meet the
needs of all students in a changing world; the community that rallied
to keep the peace and maintain the integrity of Riverside; and the
individuals who stretched their vision to see the future and became a
small part of the history of the United States.

CONTENTS

FOREWORD

By V. P. Franklin

The "quality integrated education" movement reached a new level in Riverside, California, in September 1965 with the burning of the Lowell School. In 1954 the Supreme Court's *Brown v. Board of Education* decision declared legal segregation in public education unconstitutional, and while racial barriers were soon removed in many southern school districts, politicians and other leaders in the Deep South organized campaigns of "massive resistance." In the 1950s the angry mobs attempting to prevent the "Little Rock Nine" from desegregating the all-white Central High School in September 1957 received the greatest national and international attention. In New Orleans, Louisiana, in September 1960 widespread protests were mounted after the courts ordered the enrollment of 6-year-old Ruby Bridges at the Frantz Elementary School. White parents organized a boycott and the little girl spent the entire year as the only student in the school. Rioting erupted on the campus of the University of Mississippi in Oxford in September 1962 and several people were injured when federal officials attempted to enroll James Meredith as the first African American student. The National Guard had to be called out to quell the violence.

The *Brown* decision outlawed *de jure* segregation in public education; however, in many northern and western school districts *de facto* segregation was well-entrenched due to housing patterns, but also the policies and practices of local school officials. In Chicago, New York City, Cleveland, Milwaukee, Boston, and many other cities, rather than allow African American students attending overcrowded neighborhood schools to transfer to underutilized schools in all-white areas, school officials had temporary buildings constructed in the school yards in predominantly black neighborhoods. Unfortunately, many of these "mobile classrooms" were poorly constructed and the students and teachers complained of being cold in the winter and hot in the summer and other problems. Dissatisfied parents and their supporters signed petitions, attended school board meetings, mounted protests, and ultimately organized system-wide boycotts demanding "quality integrated education."

In *No Easy Way: Integrating Riverside Schools – A Victory for Community*, Arthur L. Littleworth recounts the efforts of school leaders at the San Dimas Conference in October 1963 to address the complaints of African American parents about some of the conditions in public schools in African American and Mexican American neighborhoods. At the time Arthur Littleworth was School Board president of Riverside Unified School District (RUSD) and he knew there were excellent teachers working at these schools, but he also understood that school officials "needed to address the *perception* of unequal treatment" (p. 31). Parents and community leaders in Chicago and New York City organized citywide boycotts in the 1963-64 school year in support of their demands for quality integrated education and hundreds of "Freedom Schools" were opened to instruct students participating in the strike.

In Riverside in October 1963 under Littleworth's leadership, the RUSD mounted a "compensatory education" program aimed at African American and Mexican American students to enrich their educational experiences. The enrichment programs—academic tutoring, field trips, and lectures by African American leaders—were popular and supported by minority group leaders.

Despite the announcement of an official policy of "Open Enrollment" in the RUSD, African American parents complained that their children were not allowed to transfer from one public school to another. The goal was quality *integrated* education and the promise of Open Enrollment went unfulfilled, the "policy had been improperly administered, and that, in fact, it didn't exist at all" (p. 40). While the compensatory education programs were successful as social and cultural activities, lower test scores for minority students persisted, and many believed that integration into previously all-white school settings would improve academic outcomes.

The fire at the Lowell School early on Monday morning, 7 September 1965, forced the situation there and at the Irving and Casa Blanca schools into open debate. While the teachers were well-trained and experienced, the Lowell School was an aging facility and new schools were being built close by. The fire did great damage to several sections of the building, but some classes and the auditorium were spared. At the RUSD school board meeting the next day, the room was filled with parents wanting to learn what was going to happen. Littleworth admits that the board received bad advice from Superintendent Bruce Miller. Since only part of the building was usable, Miller recommended, and the board agreed, that Lowell students would be put on "double sessions" and plans would be made to locate spaces in other schools for displaced students.

To his credit, in *No Easy Way* Arthur Littleworth includes the story from the Riverside *Press* with the headline: "Board sets double sessions at Lowell school temporarily." The announcement was a mistake and it pushed African American parents and leaders into organizing a boycott and opening freedom schools in Riverside. But this is a story of victory. In *No Easy Way* Littleworth shares his personal perspectives, along with those of others, on the efforts to bring about the integration of the Riverside public schools. One of the major reasons why the protest was short-lived was the intelligence, fair-mindedness, and effectiveness of Arthur Littleworth. Sociologists of education have studied court-ordered public school desegregation and found that successful outcomes were much more likely in districts where local school and political leaders supported the efforts. Where effective and empathetic leaders spearheaded the implementation of voluntary or involuntary school desegregation plans, the educational and social changes were introduced without crippling controversy.

Arthur Littleworth's memoir and the remembrances of others who participated in the school integration efforts in Riverside offer insightful testimonies for understanding the history of the quality integrated education movement in the United States in the 1960s. *No Easy Way's* personal perspectives reveal how major changes were brought about in the way of doing things. Parents, community leaders, and school officials achieved an important victory; hopefully we will learn from, and be inspired by, their success.

V.P. Franklin holds a University of California Presidential Chair and is a Distinguished Professor of History and Education at UC Riverside. He edits *The Journal of African American History*, and has published over fifty scholarly articles and co-edited five books on African American history and education. He is the author of *The Education of Black Philadelphia: The Social and Educational History of a Minority Community, 1900-1950* (1979), *Black Self-Determination: A Cultural History of African American Resistance* (1984, 1992), *Living Our Stories, Telling Our Truths: Autobiography and the Making of the African American Intellectual Tradition* (1996), and *Martin Luther King, Jr.: A Biography* (1998); and co-author of *My Soul Is a Witness: A Chronology of the Civil Rights Movement, 1954-1965* (2000). He teaches the history of the Civil Rights-Black Power movements, U.S. education history, and 20th century U.S. history.

EDITOR'S PREFACE

By Dawn Hassett

No Easy Way is a local story of national import. We have this story in our hands today because of former school board president Arthur Littleworth's determination. He was determined in 1965 to integrate Riverside's schools without violence. More recently, he has been equally determined to share his experience through this memoir, despite a disabling stroke. When the Inlandia Institute received his compact but compelling account, the story, by its very nature, demanded attention.

Inlandia began to explore the best way to collaborate with Arthur Littleworth to publish a full book-length account of this vitally significant history.

The approach arose from the memoir itself. Arthur's narrative demonstrates beyond question that the integration process was comprised of many stories. In fact, it was the ability of those involved to communicate, to share points of view, and to listen to each other, which led to the resolution of the crisis. It was the multiplicity of voices and their coming together which led to the uncommon result of a community deciding to change itself for the better.

Just as the integration crisis unfolded day-by-day for Arthur Littleworth, the same incidents played out for the parents, community leaders, school board administrators, teachers, and students. By capturing their voices and recollections, it would be possible to embody some of the character of each day. History would reveal itself in real-time, participants both knowing and unknowing of each others' actions. Arthur accepted Inlandia's proposal as a natural outgrowth of his own story and I came onboard to edit the manuscript, verify sources, and conduct the interviews.

Each of the interviewees contributed with candor and thoughtfulness: Esther [Velez] Andrews, Robert Bland, Tyree Ellison, Judge Charles Field, Justice John Gabbert, Craig Goodwin, Doris [Doskocil] Haddy, Barbara [Wheelock] Hamilton, Denise Matthews, William Medina, Walter Parks, Dell Roberts, Wanda [Poole] Scruggs, Sue Strickland, Jesse Wall, Ruth [Bratten] Anderson Wilson, and Dorothy Wissler.

I am honored to have met them. They allowed me into those difficult days. They related what had happened in their streets, their homes, their workplaces, their classrooms, and their city. Every time I asked a question, the answer enriched my understanding of exactly what had transpired in Riverside in the fall of 1965. Their stories go to the heart of Arthur's memoir. The future of the community was at stake, and as the crisis evolved, voices in the community rose to uphold what was right and just—not easily, not unanimously, and not without doubt. But the participants in these pivotal events went forward in the belief that, acting together, they could make the community better.

Unsurprisingly, after 50 years, many key participants have died. The following deceased parents and community leaders were all important in achieving a peaceful resolution to the conflict: Joe Aguilar, Etienne Caroline Sr., Jean Grier, Alice Key, Don Renfro, Josephine Samuels, and Jess Ybarra. School district and city officials Ray Berry, Ben Lewis, Bruce Miller, Richard Purviance, and John Sotelo all played critical roles. A number of factors interfered with our efforts to include others who were part of the story, including Ernest Robles.

No Easy Way is the story of all of these people too.

In the course of my work, each person I talked to suggested others. Had we pursued every lead, the interviews would have overwhelmed the original memoir. We focused on those most directly involved. In this effort, we were assisted by Irving Hendrick's 1968 book, *The Development of a School Integration Plan in Riverside, California, A History and Perspective*, as well as the participants in the Lowell School Reunion in 2009.

Many people and organizations helped and we owe them thanks. Kathy Allavie, John Bender, Chuck Beaty, Terry Bridges, Jack Clarke, Jr., Rose Mayes, Jim Parsons, John Schreck, and Lew Vanderzyl helped with materials, contact information, and support. Thanks also to readers Ellen Estilai, Cati Porter, Marion Mitchell-Wilson, and Chuck Wilson.

The Press-Enterprise and Irving Hendrick generously gave permission to use materials that have greatly enriched the text. Thank you to contributors V. P. Franklin, Douglas McCulloh, and Susan Straight for their thoughtful and generous work. Walter Parks lent important historical images of Riverside schools.

It is impossible to name everyone who has assisted without omissions. If I have failed to acknowledge someone, I ask forgiveness for the oversight.

Finally, a few housekeeping notes for readers. The terms used to describe race or ethnicity vary throughout the book. When quoting from written material, the book uses the terms in the original. In interviews, the speakers are quoted directly. The interviews are not word for word transcriptions but are excerpted, with significant omissions indicated by the use of ellipses. Editor's additions are enclosed in brackets. The interviews are also edited for smoothing appropriate to the transition from spoken to written language. Finally, several of the women interviewed had different last names in 1965. Their names at that time are included in brackets.

Dawn Hassett has been a working writer all her life, employed in journalism for community-based newspapers and radio in Canada and contributing to little magazines. Before coming to California, she taught creative writing and literature for Northwest Community College. She holds a Master of Professional Writing degree from the University of Southern California. Over the past 15 years, she has edited several books and her previous Inlandia Institute projects include editing *Making Waves in Inlandia: Stories of the Inland Empire Women's Environmental Movement*. She is the author of *The Great Picture: Making the World's Largest Photograph* published by Hudson Hills Press, 2011.

INTRODUCTION

By Susan Straight

Certain names were iconic during my childhood, my young adulthood, and even after I was married in my native Riverside. I would hear these names from teachers, from family members on Riverside's Eastside, from elders in the community. Art Littleworth was a hero and friend to many of the people I grew up with here – my mother and father-in-law, their friends, pastors and activists. Along with Dell Roberts, Judge John Gabbert, Pastor Jesse Wall, Henry Blanco, Horace Jackson and many other people, Art Littleworth changed history in Riverside, and that helped my fellow classmates and me become who we are.

When I interviewed him in 2012 for a story about Riverside's Eastside, Art and Peggy Littleworth, along with John Gabbert and his daughter Katie Smith, told stories which brought the days and weeks described in this memoir to vivid life. The burning of Lowell School, but also the way Littleworth himself had grown up, how he saw the world after his military service, his time in college and law school, and then in 1950s Riverside.

But this history he described was also very personal for me, because so many of my relatives and friends were directly affected by his intelligent bravery, legal decisions, and staunch persistence in the face of frightening opposition.

The day after Lowell School burned, John Bennett was supposed to begin first grade, and instead of arriving at that largely segregated school, he did his first day of lessons in a room on the second floor of the Orange Valley Lodge, under the direction of an older white man who had arrived to teach him. "A Freedom School," it was called – just like the ones in the South, where civil rights battles were fierce. A photo published in *The Press-Enterprise* showed the volunteer helping Bennett read a book– a scene that could have been out of Mississippi. John Bennett is married now to my former sister-in-law.

That same day, while the Lowell buildings were still smoldering rubble, Art Littleworth was already thinking about what to do. "It was a time of anger," he told me softly that day in 2012. Should Riverside's schools integrate? Littleworth was president of the Riverside School Board. "I thought we should be one city," he said, at his house in a hundred-year-old orange grove – on Victoria Avenue, only a few miles from where Lowell had burned. "One city."

Littleworth drew up a plan to bus black and Mexican-American students from Irving and Lowell Schools, which were nearly all minority enrollment, to schools throughout Riverside Over the next year, the integration plan was expanded to Emerson and Casa Blanca Schools. This wasn't an easy decision – he sat on a stage, while invective and questions were hurled with equal force. As Judge John Gabbert recalled at Littleworth's house, sitting beside his friend, "Riverside had plenty of people who never wanted their children to mix. There was a strong Ku Klux Klan presence here in the 1920s – that's sometimes forgotten, but there was animus and distrust." Art Littleworth's stance was brave – he actually slept at the houses of various friends, for protection from possible retribution.

But Riverside became the first school district in America to voluntarily desegregate, without a court order forcing it to do so. Not easy for many of the children, or their teachers, who were bused away from the Eastside – but life changed for those children, and for their teachers.

Susan Strickland told me, "I was teaching at Emerson then, and they took two of us teachers out of Emerson and had us ride the bus with the kids. I went to Highland. I had second grade. Lydia Wilson was probably in sixth grade, and one day early on, her teacher used the n-word. Oh, Marcille Wilson was upset. She called me right away and said, I'm headed up there to that principal in the morning." Marcille Wilson's family lived on Michael Street; she ran a successful hair salon. She spoke her mind, strongly, at Highland.

Marcille Wilson's granddaughter, Aashanique Wilson, is now studying photography at Riverside Community College. She hopes to document life in Southern California, and it has to be believed that her education was different from what it could have been, because of Art Littleworth.

I was there, in kindergarten at Highland Elementary. My mother walked me the first day, and I walked the one block alone after that. I saw the big yellow buses, and wished for seven years that I could ride a bus with my face pressed to the window, as I'd seen on television. But because of Lowell School and desegregation, I never knew classrooms that were not mixed almost equally with white, black and Mexican-American students. For all those years, we were together on playground swings and sports teams, in the auditorium at Highland where I was the only white girl on my sixth grade dance team (I was so clumsy that Janet Aubert, Tyra Tatum, and Toni Winston had me in charge of the record player while they did a routine to "ABC" by the Jackson Five, but we did have matching dance outfits).

The truth is simple: I would not be the writer and professor I am today without the experiences I had during my entire public school education in Riverside. Sitting with Art Littleworth that day, it all came back so vividly to me, and I watched the animated hands of this man who'd orchestrated change.

We all went to the new University Junior High, built in the orange groves equidistant from several neighborhoods. We began to fall in love. I met my future husband there, and hundreds of schoolchildren met their future spouses or lifelong friends in school. We spent the majority of our waking hours, as young people, in school, and then we worked together. Integration, as it came about here, is visible every day. And that is the legacy of Art Littleworth, Dell Roberts, Jesse Wall, Susan Strickland, Henry Blanco, who was a teacher there at University, and many others. Our children all attend school together now – their skins and hair and voices the mélange of the future before the rest of America had figured it out.

Susan Straight has published eight novels and two books for children. Her new novel *Between Heaven and Here* (McSweeney's) is the final book in the Rio Seco trilogy. *Take One Candle Light a Room* (Anchor Books) was named one of the best books of 2010 by *The Washington Post* and *The Los Angeles Times*, and *A Million Nightingales* (Anchor Books) was a Finalist for the Los Angeles Times Book Prize in 2006. *Highwire Moon* was a Finalist for the 2001 National Book Award. "The Golden Gopher," published in *Los Angeles Noir*, won the 2008 Edgar Award for Best Mystery Story. Her stories and essays have appeared in *The O Henry Prize Stories, Best American Short Stories, The New York Times, The Los Angeles Times, Harpers, McSweeney's, The Believer, Salon, Zoetrope, Black Clock*, and elsewhere. She has been awarded The Lannan Prize for Fiction, a Guggenheim Fellowship, and the Gold Medal for Fiction from the Commonwealth Club of California. She is Distinguished Professor of Creative Writing at UC Riverside. With Douglas McCulloh, she writes for KCET, and their show *More Dreamers of the Golden Dream* featured stories of Riverside's Eastside. She was born in Riverside, California, where she lives with her family, whose history is featured on susanstraight.com.

Mission Inn - Riverside Calif-

CHAPTER 1 — PROLOGUE

Some fifty years ago, on September 7, 1965, well before dawn, Riverside's Lowell School was gutted by fire. It was clearly arson, but it has never been discovered who set the blaze.

Riverside, California, located about 50 miles east of Los Angeles, was a community of nearly 135,000 in 1965. It was founded in 1870 by John W. North, a friend of President Lincoln and a staunch abolitionist. North's advertisement for settlers in California read, "We wish to form a colony of intelligent, industrious and enterprising people (who are willing to invest $1000 in the purchase of land) so that each one's industry will help to promote his neighbor's interests as well as his own . . . we expect to have Schools, Churches, Lyceum, Public Library, etc. at a very early day."[1]

Riverside's location was ideal. In 1965, it was isolated from the suburbs of Los Angeles by about 20 miles of vineyards and orange trees. Within one hour's driving time you could go to Los Angeles, ski in the 10,000-foot San Bernardino mountains, enjoy Palm Springs and the desert, or swim in the Pacific ocean at Laguna Beach. Riverside was a city of trees and the famous Mission Inn. The Inn was the center of Riverside's culture and was visited by many Hollywood celebrities and national figures. Presidents Theodore Roosevelt, William Howard Taft, and Richard Nixon; actors Bette Davis, Ginger Rogers, and Cary Grant; and notables

---

1.   Patterson, Tom. *A Colony for California* (Riverside: The Museum Press of the Riverside Museum Associates, 1996), 19.

Booker T. Washington, Amelia Earhart, John Muir, Andrew Carnegie, and Houdini were among the celebrities who visited the Inn over the years. Riverside was also the home of the navel orange industry. The first navel orange tree was imported to Riverside in about 1873. Navels do not have seeds and so new trees are grafted from old trees. The original navel orange tree, the ancestor of the navel orange trees in California, is still alive and planted in the middle of the city, tended carefully by University of California, Riverside scientists.

Election ad 1958, Arthur L. Littleworth with children Todd (left) and Anne (right), running for his first election to the Board of Education in November 1958. He initially joined the board on March 17, 1958, to fill the unexpired term of a member who had resigned.

My wife, Evie, and I settled in Riverside in 1950. Both of us were raised in Los Angeles and intended to go back there upon my graduation from Yale Law School. I had received an offer from one of the prestigious large law firms in Los Angeles, but three years of living in New England had left its mark. We liked the smaller community of New Haven instead of the big city. We decided that Riverside was a good place to raise a family and it provided a unique opportunity for public service.

At the close of the school year in June 1965, the Riverside Unified School District served about 25,000 students. Within the elementary schools, approximately seventeen percent of students were minorities. But three elementary schools were segregated because their neighborhoods were also segregated. Irving, Lowell, and Casa Blanca had almost one hundred percent minority enrollment. All of the other schools in the district had at least some minority students.

Just before the opening of school in September 1965, Lowell School was burned down. The Lowell fire started about 2 a.m., but the fire department was not called until 4 a.m. The fire destroyed about half of the school—the old main building that held six or seven classrooms, the administration offices, and the library. Some new classrooms were left standing and unharmed. The population of Lowell School was virtually all African-American and Mexican-American children.

I was president of the School Board from 1962 to 1972,[2] so the burning of Lowell School and the crisis which followed is firmly etched in my memory. These shocking events came to Riverside about three weeks after the embers had cooled down from the Watts riots and fires in Los Angeles.

2. I was a member of the School Board from 1958-1972. The other members of the School Board in 1965 were: Margaret Heers, active in community affairs; Evelyn Kendrick, wife of a UCR professor; Dr. Vernon Stern, a UCR professor; and B. Rae Sharp, a leading certified public accountant.

Left: The Press, *September 7, 1965. "Search for Cause—Investigators begin tedious digging through still hot debris to discover cause of early morning fire at Lowell School. Chief Charles Brague of the Fire Prevention Bureau directs search. Using large spoons they dug up molten glass and a jar lid in hole beneath window where fire started." The Press staff photo by Bob Ringquist.*

Above: Los Angeles Fire Department photograph of the Watts Riots.

Top right: Los Angeles police officers detain Watts residents on the street.

Below right: Soldiers of 40th Armored Division-California National Guard direct traffic away from an area of South Central Los Angeles burning during the Watts Riots.

The Watts riots of August 1965 broke out as the result of the racial tensions between the community and the police. The riots shook the whole nation and lasted for six days, with looting, vandalism, and fires resulting in the deaths of 34 people, almost 900 injuries, and the destruction or damage of almost 1,000 buildings. About 14,000 troops of the National Guard were deployed to restore order. The mob's slogan was "Burn, Baby, Burn." Certainly, a question in the minds of many was, would that slogan be heard in Riverside? As the fires raged, the rioters blocked firemen from doing their job. Firemen were fired upon by snipers. Arson and rampant looting were mostly confined to white-owned stores and businesses in the rioters' own neighborhoods, the South Central part of Los Angeles. There were no fires in Hollywood or Beverly Hills.

Mainstream white Americans viewed the rioters as criminals destroying and looting their own neighborhoods. Many in the black community, however, saw the rioters as taking part in an uprising against an oppressive system. The McCone Commission, headed by former CIA director John A. McCone, in a December 1965 report, identified the root causes of the riots to be high unemployment, poor schools, and inferior living conditions in Watts. But Martin Luther King, Jr., remarked, "What did Watts accomplish but the death of 34 Negroes and injury to thousands more? What did it profit the Negro to burn down the stores and factories in which he sought employment? The way of riots is not a way of progress, but a blind alley of death and destruction which wreaks its havoc hardest against the rioters themselves." The Watts riots were the backdrop of the drama as the Riverside crisis unfolded.

I was reminded of the Lowell fire in December 2006, when a man approached me at the reception following the memorial service at Calvary Presbyterian Church for Wayne Holcomb, a former City Council member and a long-time director of the Western Municipal Water District. He said, "You don't know me, but I know you well. Most people," he continued, "don't know how much this town owes you. It would have been burned down without you." It turned out that he had been the police officer who was the arson investigator of the Lowell fire, and he was assigned to me as a plain-clothes officer to "watch my back." He remembered well some of the tense mass meetings with out-of-town agitators yelling out hate and trying to stir up the crowd. He said that he would stand close behind these groups, watching carefully to see that things did not get out of control. But despite the ugly things shouted at me, he said, "You always remained calm, and eventually you would get the crowd to quiet down." Our conversation was brief as other people at the reception moved in on us, but I shook his hand and expressed my profound thanks. I didn't get his name. I should have, because the community, and I too, owe him a great deal of gratitude.

JUSTICE JOHN GABBERT
COMMUNITY LEADER

Born in 1909, John Gabbert moved to Riverside with his parents in 1912. His father, J. R. Gabbert, purchased the *Enterprise* newspaper, and John grew up working there. He graduated from Boalt School of Law in 1934. He served first as deputy district attorney and then, in 1938, joined Raymond and Eugene Best at their law practice, which became Best Best and Gabbert.

He served on the board of the Riverside School District from 1946 to 1949. As president of the Citizens University Committee, he was instrumental in bringing a campus of the University of California to Riverside. In 1949, he was appointed as a judge in the Superior Court of Riverside County, where he served until 1970, when he was named associate justice of the California Appellate Court, Fourth Appellate District. He retired in 1974.

Justice John Gabbert: *I think that what you have to do is go back in history and think about how Riverside viewed integration and assimilation and contact with other groups. The pioneers who founded Riverside were doing it on a partial basis of the idea of the "City on the Hill," that Riverside was going to be a law abiding city, a place of refuge.* *["City upon the Hill" was a Pilgrim metaphor for the world's scrutiny of New England colonies and whether they would live up to their pledge of becoming model communities for the rest of the world.]*

There was a considerable Transcendental foundation in Riverside's formation, by Judge North [the abolitionist who founded Riverside as a utopian community in 1870] and others. They looked at Riverside as being something special . . . in the earliest days, back in the 1870s, 80s.

But in the 20s, the Ku Klux Klan came to Riverside and started a big outdoor religious revival, and they had a lot of pretty powerful, wild-eyed speakers. [An expanded platform that targeted Catholics, Jews, and foreigners in addition to blacks helped Klan membership balloon to approximately 5 million nationwide in the 1920s. Their strategy, called "the decade," required each Klan member to recruit ten people to vote for Klan candidates in local elections. Candidates ran on policies of fundamentalism, devout patriotism, and white supremacy, making speeches blasting bootleggers, motion pictures, and intellectuals. In Riverside, the One Hundred Per Cent American League, an organization whose menacing accusations bore many similarities to the Klan, supported Mayor Edward Dighton, an ardent prohibitionist.]

I remember, my father was editor of the Enterprise *newspaper, J.R. Gabbert. He was against the Ku Klux Klan like nobody else was. He was writing articles against the Klan and they were coming on strong. They were going to take over the city. They elected the mayor and two city councilmen. If they got another councilman, they would be running the city.*

My dad strongly opposed them, and The Press *newspaper strongly opposed them, too. I remember going to meetings at night, of the Klan. My dad would take me. We would stand out on the edges of the crowd. We would not participate but he wanted to see what was going on.*

So my father wrote an editorial about the Ku Klux Klan, and the mayor, Mr. Dighton, then filed a criminal libel against my father. The local judges recused themselves and the Supreme Court of the state sent a judge out from Los Angeles. There was such a crowd at the courthouse they couldn't let everyone in, so they moved it over to the auditorium at the Elk's club so they had more room.

When the attorney for my father made his argument, the judge threw the case out. . . . I remember sitting around the dining room table that evening and they were all happy he had won the case, and my mother said, "But Ray, how much did it cost you?" He said, "Well, I had to pay [my lawyer] today a thousand dollars." And I said, "How long did he talk?"

. . . Gabbert continued on page 7

Out of this turmoil in 1965, Riverside became the first large city in the nation to voluntarily develop a full-scale integration plan. This, without a federal court intervention, and without any "white flight" which characterized many of the forced busing programs that occurred in 1968 and later. The Riverside community could be justly proud of its accomplishments—a tribute to the Riverside abolitionist founder, John Wesley North.

My conversation with the former officer took me back to 1965 and reminded me of the true violence that Riverside was then facing. At that time emotions ran high, and I felt then that details of the story might cause further unrest. Now, however, the situation has changed, and the full story of the frightening days of 1965, and the lessons learned from it, might contribute to binding Riverside into "one people."

I decided then that I would write my recollection of Riverside's school integration when I retired from my legal career. That time came sooner than I had expected when, in January 2008, I suffered a severe stroke. I could not walk, talk, or write, but my memory was fine. Now, after countless hours of physical therapy sessions, and a partial recovery, I am able to write this memoir and to relate the experience of that pivotal time in Riverside's history.

Most people mark the Lowell fire as the beginning of Riverside's school integration efforts. Certainly this was the beginning of a crisis that was unprecedented in Riverside's history. But I am not at all sure that our reaction to the fire, and the ultimate integration efforts, would have been the same but for developments that began years earlier.

Above: Lowell School, 1959. Teacher Barbara [Wheelock] Hamilton's fourth grade class.

Gabbert continued from page 5

And my dad said, "About 20 minutes." I said, "You had to pay him a thousand dollars for 20 minutes? Boy, that's what I'd like to do."

[But even with this experience, Judge Gabbert was not fully aware of what black residents of California faced on a daily basis.] In 1942, before I went in the army, I had a client who was a black man . . . a pretty smart guy, who got the shoeshine concessions in all the barbershops. There were about six or seven and every one had two or three chairs to get your shoes shined. . . . Danny Culpepper was his name.

Later on, about the time we got into the war, Riverside was the headquarters of March Field, Camp Hahn, Camp Anza, and Mira Loma Quartermaster Depot, and General Patton was the director of training for the desert troops training to go into North Africa down in the Coachella Valley. The net result was that all these servicemen were around Riverside, and they had time off now and then, and there wasn't anything for them to do.

So Danny Culpepper, who had been making money with his shoe shining business, got busy and organized two clubs to appeal to the common soldier and the dark soldier. . . . The Culpepper clubs were always running into fights, difficulties, and finally the Board of Alcoholic Beverage Control cancelled his license, which put him out of business. I took an appeal . . . [to] the whole Board of Equalization in Sacramento. So he and I planned to go up there and present our case there, which we did . . . and we won the case.

My client was very happy. So I said we might as well start out for home, [but first] we'd stop and get something to eat. He said, "Well, where are you going?" I said that there were a lot of nice drive-ins around. . . . Those days at drive-ins, the young ladies came out on skates with a tray. He said, "No, when they see me in the car, they won't serve you."

I said, "You're wrong," but he was right. We stopped at one of the better ones in Sacramento, and a gal came out and looked in the car, and skated away. . . . She never did come back.

He said, "I'll just go in a grocery store and get some crackers and cheese. That's what we have to do." That was the first time it was ever brought to my attention. It's hard to believe but that's true. . . . I had never had any contact with the full situation and scale of integration and lack of it. We went to another place and I think we got turned down there too. We did get something, somewhere.

We continued and at six o'clock, we were in Tulare. My wife was from Tulare and I had been there many, many, many times. And when I was there I always stayed at the Johnson Hotel. I said, "We'll go over to the Johnson, they'll fix us up."

So we went over to the Johnson, and they said, "Sorry, Mr. Gabbert, we're redecorating, we haven't any rooms." It wasn't true.

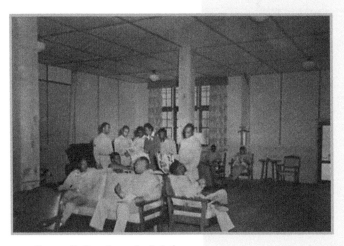

Above: Enlisted men's club for African-American soldiers at Camp Anza in Riverside during World War II. The armed forces were segregated until 1948.

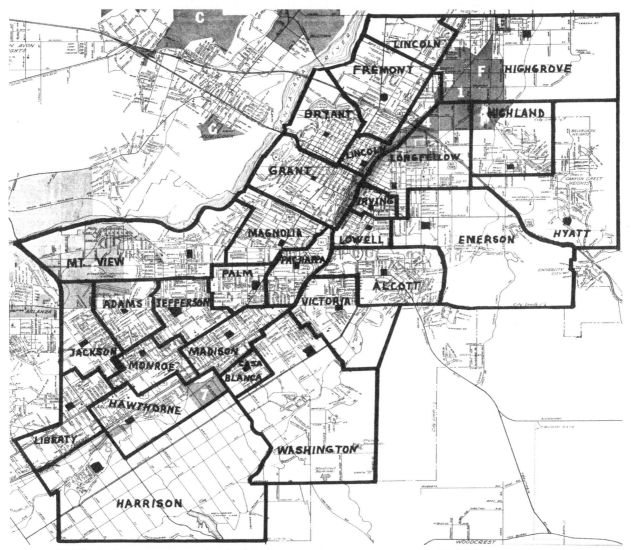

Above: School attendance area boundaries for the 1964–1965 school year (Hendrick, The Development of a School Integration Plan in Riverside, California, A History and Perspective. *245).*

Irving School 1891–1955

CHAPTER 2 — MINORITY SCHOOLS

Irving, Lowell and Casa Blanca Schools

In 1965, the Riverside Unified School District served about 25,000 students. Of these, approximately seventeen percent were minority students in the elementary schools. But three elementary schools—Irving, Lowell, and Casa Blanca—had almost one hundred percent minority enrollment. The other schools in the District— elementary, middle, and high schools—all had some minority students.

Irving School

Irving School was constructed in 1891 and served Riverside's historic "Eastside," a community comprised primarily of African-American and Mexican-American residents. It was located at Victoria Avenue and 14th Street, and today is the site of Lincoln Continuation School.

It was originally referred to as the "black" school, as opposed to the "white" Lowell School. Constructed in 1911, Lowell was located at the corner of Victoria Avenue and Cridge Street, less than half a mile from Irving school. Neighborhoods change over time, and in 1965 Irving School had an enrollment of 180 African-American and 140 Mexican-American students.

In 1952, as part of a five-year building program, the school administration proposed replacement of four classrooms at Irving, and went further to say, "consideration should be given to replacement of this structure in its entirety." A letter signed by five leading citizens of the area proposed eight new classrooms instead of four.[3] A subsequent letter from the Eastside Citizens Committee recommended that an entirely new school be built at Irving. Riverside was growing. New schools were being constructed and the parents at Irving were concerned that their school would be left out of the reconstruction. The Irving community affirmed the neighborhood school concept despite the fact that it would result in segregation because it would serve a predominantly minority neighborhood. Neighborhood schools had many virtues. Students were with their friends, and could walk to school. Students are more apt to participate in after-school activities. And parents, too, are more apt to participate in the classroom activities of their children. In short, a neighborhood school meant "our" school.

The result was that in 1954 the first six new classrooms were constructed, and by 1956 the entire reconstruction, including razing the old school, had been completed. The buildings at Irving were at that time among the finest in the District.

Irving School administration building after reconstruction.

---

3.   Included among the signed were L.B. Moss, president of the NAACP, and Jesse M. Carlos, president of the Latin American Club.

DOROTHY WISSLER
RESEARCHER

Dorothy Wissler's medical education, in addition to her bachelor's in history and doctorate in education administration, includes degrees as a registered nurse, public health nurse, nurse practitioner, and a master's degree from Loma Linda University. She was also a member of the university's first class of graduating nurse practitioners. She retired as the director of the Student Health Center at San Bernardino Valley College.

Her doctoral studies at the University of California, Riverside examined the structure and effect of decentralized decision-making as an organizational model for school districts. The major focus of her research was Riverside Unified School District under Ray Berry.

Dorothy Wissler: *Bruce Miller was a typical [upper middle class man], well accepted . . . comfortable, happy to be with people, his equals, and not even aware of how un-equal some felt. At that time, white males lived in a beautifully spun cocoon; their fathers had been the same. Culture can actually ruin you because you are a product of it.*

Miller was unable to change, probably even unaware that a change was necessary, because he always felt like he was doing good. [However, the minority community had] needs he didn't understand—their longings, their feelings of inequality. It wasn't just their feelings, it was actually how they were treated. They were living two different lives. They might as well have been in two different countries.

Littleworth and Berry were working toward making things more equal. They probably [were not really thinking about the fact that] the people who were dissatisfied had been told that [those in charge] were working toward change for them for 200 years. And so, Littleworth and Berry couldn't see the gradual overwhelming dissatisfaction that couldn't be held in bounds any longer. Many promises had been given over many years, but none of them had borne fruit. So maybe [because they had begun to discuss integration in 1962], Littleworth and Berry and the board had actually, unbeknown to themselves, created the freedom for the crisis. These parents . . . may have felt a little more free to say, "No, we want it now."

The genius of both Berry and Littleworth is that they were a bridge. What Mr. Berry did, with Mr. Littleworth, was change the structure of the district from a pyramid with the board at the top, [to one where] the total thrust should be on the child—so much so that if anyone asked someone who worked there, "What is this school district about?"—the immediate answer would be—"to educate every child who comes to us to the best of their ability."

Something happened in Riverside. Littleworth and Berry didn't think that certain children could learn and certain children couldn't learn, that the children who lived "down the hill" couldn't learn and the children who lived "up the hill" could learn. That was the ingrained thinking of people in many school districts, but Berry and Littleworth felt that every child could learn. So every child was equal in value to the district.

From the review of the literature I did, desegregation failed in every single large district, like New York, Chicago. They may have done some moving of children about, but every single schoolroom was not desegregated. In Riverside, the effort was made to desegregate every schoolroom. That's a big difference from desegregating a district.

From the minute he came to that school district, Berry had a vision of what he wanted to do, and that was to educate all the children. In order to do that, there had to be changes and he didn't know how, but he wanted input from everybody. And Art was open enough and brilliant enough, and morally so upright, that he wanted to actualize what we all say. I think Art was definitely a hero, because he was the leader of that school board.

11

Lowell School

The attendance area at Lowell included the area north of the Victoria Golf Course and some of the wealthiest households in Riverside, along Prince Albert Drive. Originally, the student enrollment was all white, but gradually minorities moved into the area. Also the opening of Victoria and Emerson Schools, in 1955 and 1956 respectively, siphoned off some of the white students from Lowell. By 1960 the enrollment at Lowell was approximately 50 percent white, 50 percent minority. The upcoming opening of the new Alcott School in 1961 would doom Lowell to become a minority school, and the School District for the first time was forced to consider a problem of *de facto* segregation.[4] The Board began in 1961 to consider integration, among the possible alternatives, for the future of Lowell School.

A well-drafted 1961 petition from a citizens' group at Lowell wanted "their children to have the privileges and the responsibilities which go with the right to attend and be fully educated in an integrated school." At the Board meeting on May 15, 1961, Dean Newell, principal spokesman for the group, limited his appeals to only two requests: a stay of the Alcott School boundary decision which removed more white students from Lowell School, and the formation of a study committee to

4.   *De facto* means segregation arising from changes in residential housing, not legal segregation caused by laws requiring or permitting racial segregation.

Above: Teacher Doris [Doskocil] Haddy's 1960–1961 third grade class of 22 students at Lowell School is relatively integrated with 60 percent minority students and 40 percent majority students.

Right: After the opening of Alcott School in 1961–1962, her class is virtually segregated with 88 percent minority students.

LOWELL SCHOOL
Riverside, California
February, 1962

Mr. Richard Purviance
Principal

Mrs. Doris Doskocil
Third Grade

consider the entire problem of *de facto* segregation. The petition went on to say that "Lowell School has been a model integrated school, a credit not only to the city, its school officials, and the Lowell principal and his staff, but also to the nation and a world in great need of examples of how to live together. Our group is proud to be a part of such a school, and those of us who are living in an integrated neighborhood are morally proud of this fact."

In response to the petition, a community group was formed consisting of blacks, Mexican Americans, and whites. Three members of the School Board were also on the committee: B. Rae Sharp, Carolyn Diffenbaugh,[5] and me as chairman. The group was known as the Lowell Study Committee and it dealt with many of the ramifications of integration, not in terms of Lowell alone, but in Riverside in general. The Committee considered several plans: transporting additional Caucasian students into Lowell; adjusting boundaries to include more Caucasians at Lowell; abolishing school boundaries; making Lowell into a gifted school; transporting all fourth, fifth, and sixth grade pupils from Lowell to other Riverside schools; making this option applicable to Irving also; and finally, abandoning certain schools and the controlled dispersing of minority group pupils to other Riverside schools. This alternative was a precursor to what was actually done in 1965.

In the end, I presented the Committee's recommendations to the School Board on June 16, 1961: "We feel that the best solution to the Lowell problem would be one of controlled dispersal of the upper grades into as large a number of Riverside schools as is feasible." The Committee's second recommendation was to form a citywide committee for study "of the overall problem of integration in regards to schools, housing and recreation." The Riverside City Council offered no support for a citywide study, and it was never done. Neither the NAACP nor any civil rights group was involved in the study or the Committee's recommendation.

The School Board ordered Superintendent Bruce Miller to react to the Committee's recommendations. He considered the cost of all alternatives, the support for the neighborhood schools, and the lack of community support for mandating integration, and he suggested an alternate plan. His proposal was an "Open Enrollment" of the fifth and sixth grades at Lowell, allowing children to go to other schools. The plan would preserve the principle of the neighborhood school while providing integration experiences for those pupils whose parents desired them. The principle of Open Enrollment was a progressive idea at that time, and reasonably satisfactory to everyone. However, few Lowell students took advantage of the Open Enrollment policy.

The Superintendent's plan was adopted. However, it did not prevent Lowell from becoming a segregated school.

---

5. She was later the first president of the Board of Trustees of Riverside City College when the college was split off from the Riverside Board of Education.

Casa Blanca School

Casa Blanca was far different from the Irving and Lowell communities. Sometime around 1900, a growing number of Mexicans replaced the Chinese workers in the groves and packinghouses in Riverside's booming citrus industry and established the settlement of Casa Blanca. By 1965 Casa Blanca was a distinctly Mexican-American barrio in Riverside, with Spanish being spoken primarily even by the people who were born in Riverside.

In 1913 the first school in Casa Blanca was set up in an abandoned warehouse, which offered only kindergarten and first grade classes. In 1923 Mabra Madden was appointed as the first principal of Casa Blanca School, and 41 years later he was still there as principal. Mr. Madden was far more than a principal of an elementary school, and Casa Blanca School was more than an elementary school. Madden was the unofficial mayor of Casa Blanca. He was a counselor, amateur attorney, and notary public; he helped people find jobs or directed them to proper public or private agencies for help; and occasionally he paid bills out of his own funds. His school was the center of community life in Casa Blanca.

Casa Blanca was a tight community that extended from Lincoln Avenue to Indiana Avenue and on both sides of Madison Avenue. Its school was 100 percent minority, mostly Mexican Americans. It was common in Southern California to have an isolated Mexican-American community with segregated schools. It was a community of choice based on residence. The residents of Casa Blanca took pride in the community, and liked their neighborhood school. It was not surprising that parents in Casa Blanca took little notice of the nationwide changes that were occurring towards the education of black children.

Conclusion

The afternoon of the Lowell fire, just five years after the Lowell Study Committee report, black leaders petitioned the School Board demanding that both Irving and Lowell be closed, "reassigning their students to other schools in the area" where enrollment was less than 10 percent minority. The petition said nothing about Casa Blanca. The reversal from neighborhood schools to integrated schools was led by black parents in the Irving and Lowell school communities. But when the Board of Education considered ending segregation in all elementary schools it had to consider Casa Blanca. The parents in the Casa Blanca area, however, initially didn't want any changes in their school.

The plaintiffs in Brown v. Board of Education.

CHAPTER 3 — THE STATE OF THE LAW

Brown v. Board of Education

In 1954 the U.S. Supreme Court decided the case of *Brown v. Board of Education of Topeka*, 347 U.S. 483, and its effect on public education was monumental. The decision, written by Chief Justice Warren, was unanimous.[6] The Court held "that in the field of public education the doctrine of 'separate but equal' has no place. Separate educational facilities are inherently unequal." The plaintiffs were, by reason of the segregation complained of, deprived of the equal protection of the laws guaranteed by the Fourteenth Amendment.

The case involved four states—Kansas, South Carolina, Virginia, and Delaware. The plaintiffs (children) were denied admission to "white" schools under laws that required or permitted segregation according to race. The four states had been following the law announced in the 1896 case of *Plessy v. Ferguson*,[7] 163 U.S. 537. For some 50 years, separate but equal had been the foundation of segregated schools in the country.

---

6. One of the participants on the winning side was Thurgood Marshall who later became a distinguished Justice of the U.S. Supreme Court.

7. *Plessy v. Ferguson* involved not education but transportation, but was later extended to education.

But in 1954, the Supreme Court said,

> We must look instead to the effect of segregation itself on public education . . . To separate them from others of similar age and qualification solely because of their race generates a feeling of inferiority as to status in the community that may affect their hearts and minds in a way unlikely ever to be undone.

The Court also quoted from the lower court in the Kansas case:

> Segregation of white and colored children in public schools has a detrimental effect upon the colored children. The impact is greater when it has the sanction of the law; for the policy of separating the races is usually interpreted as denoting the inferiority of the Negro group. A sense of inferiority affects the motivation of a child to learn. Segregation with the sanction of law, therefore, has a tendency to [retard] the educational and mental development of Negro children and to deprive them of some of the benefits they would receive in a racially integrated school system.

The Supreme Court held second hearings one year later dealing with complexities arising from the transition to a system of public education freed of racial discrimination. (*Brown v. Board of Education*, 349 U.S. 294). The burden rested upon school districts to establish the amount of time necessary for good faith compliance "at the earliest practicable date." The decision allowed school districts to consider problems arising from the physical condition of the school plant, the school transportation system, personnel, revision of attendance areas, and revision of local laws and regulations which might be necessary to solving the problems. It was in this second decision (1955) that the Supreme Court laid down the rule that public education must be on a racially nondiscriminatory basis "with all deliberate speed."

The first real measure of the federal government's efforts to enforce the *Brown* decision came in 1957. Arkansas Governor Orval Faubus sent National Guard troops to block nine black students from entering Central High School in Little Rock. President Eisenhower responded by ordering in the Army's crack 101st Airborne Division to support the Supreme Court's decision. That division had parachuted behind the German lines on D-Day, June 6, 1944. The federal troops formed a ring around the black students as they entered the high school. There was no violence, but the enforcement power of the Supreme Court was clear.

This was the state of the law upon my appointment to the Riverside Board of Education in 1958. We in California thought that racial segregation in public schools was mainly a problem in "the South." I thought the problems were the result of laws that required or permitted racial segregation, and we had no such laws in the West. For Riverside, segregation was not the dominant issue in 1958. Rather, the primary concerns were the city's explosive growth and the American response to Sputnik and Russia which had put the first man in space.

Growth and Federal Financing in Riverside

Between 1950 and 1960, the population of Riverside almost doubled from 46,764 to 84,332, and by 1965 the population had reached 133,200. The School District constructed seven new elementary schools during the 1950s. We split off Riverside City College from the Riverside school district; turned over the Polytechnic (Poly) High campus to the new College district;[8] and began constructing two new high schools—the replacement of Poly, at Victoria and Central Avenues, and John W. North, located at Blaine and Chicago Avenues.

The "old" Poly campus was located next to Riverside's historic "downtown," but schools were needed in the expanding residential areas. Orange trees were giving way to subdivisions. Poly was placed in a former orange grove and served the central part of Riverside. North High School was located in the new University of California, Riverside area serving the northern part of the city. Ramona High School, also built in the 1950s, served the southern part of Riverside. The old Poly High School site had freeway access and with an adult population who could drive served nicely as the site of Riverside Community College.

Riverside held bond elections in 1954, 1956, 1957, 1960, and 1963 for the construction of new schools and the acquisition of new sites. And there was a nationwide search for new teachers. Recruitment efforts were made in the all-black colleges in the South.

Besides growth, the other dominating interest was the public and government response to the Russians putting the first man in space ahead of the United States. That response led to a rapid energy surge in our space program and, incidentally, fuelled Southern California's growth through the aerospace industry.

But there was a far more fundamental change in our government: the financing of public education. While the cost of elementary and high schools had been traditionally a local matter, Congress thought that federal financing was needed also. Millions of dollars were spent on incentive grants and today, of course, billions of dollars of federal money is spent every year on public education. There was a nationwide demand to upgrade our schools, particularly in the areas of math and science. I remember one of the first grants that Riverside received. It was used to put microscopes in all the science rooms in our middle schools.

Riversiders voted a tax increase to improve school programs,[9] and together with federal funding, this brought about many changes—potentially leading to academic improvements. During those years, Riverside experimented with the "new math" curriculum, changes in the way reading was taught, the introduction of foreign

---

8. The old Poly campus (on Magnolia Avenue) was jointly occupied by the high school and the college. The college was sometimes referred to as grades 13 and 14.

9. School districts had the power to tax, with the approval of the voters. Later, the law was changed so that school districts no longer had the power to tax but received funds from the state.

languages in the elementary grades, classes for the gifted students, the expansion of summer school, teacher training, and a host of other innovations.

In all, there was an earnest and successful effort to improve education, but I felt we did not get our money's worth with the billions of federal dollars spent on education over the years.

The federal nationwide system was based mainly on applications of individual school districts and grants from the federal government. Applications were generally made on an experimental basis. In reading, for example, what if reading were taught by different techniques, by smaller classes, by more time, by different textbooks, by reading specialists, etc.? There were countless grants for reading, but there was little federal determination about which programs or approaches were successful and which were failures.

It could be said that we still don't know the reason why America is behind most of the industrial countries of the world in reading, math, and science. Is the reason for the gap that foreign students go to school more months a year? Or spend more hours per day in school? Or have more money spent on education? Or better teaching? Or more discipline? Or more parent involvement? Or more respect for learning? Or a combination of these factors and others? The federal government's program provides conflicting analysis and few answers.

Gerrymandering to Achieve Segregation

During my years on the School Board the federal courts had ruled consistently against laws that required or allowed segregation. Later courts extended those prohibitions to school districts that deliberately "gerrymandered" to effect segregation. (*Taylor v. Board of Education of New Rochelle*, (1961) 191 F. Supp. 181). Whether the segregation was caused by law or the gerrymandering of the school districts, it is called by the courts the "*de jure*" system, and is a violation of *Brown v. Board of Education*. Once the *de jure* segregated condition is found, the courts have a broad discretion to fashion a remedy, for example to change attendance zones, or implement busing, or pairing of schools. (*Swann v. Charlotte-Mecklenburg Board of Education*, (1971) 402 U.S. 1).

In New Rochelle, New York, for example, the Board of Education in 1961 carved out white students from the attendance area of the predominately black Lincoln School and transferred them to predominately white Daniel Webster School. When black families started to move into the Daniel Webster area, the black students were transferred from Daniel Webster to predominantly black Lincoln School, gerrymandering the school boundaries to effect segregation. In the New Rochelle case, the court's remedy to this type of gerrymandering was simple: allow the Lincoln students to transfer to any elementary school in the district, as long as the parents provided the necessary transportation.

If the court required very little from New Rochelle, the other extreme of court remedies for segregation was Detroit and its suburbs. In 1970 the Detroit enrollment was about 64 percent black and 35 percent white. There the court found numerous *de jure* conditions resulting from the state and local school districts deliberately creating segregation. The trial judge also found that City of Detroit public schools could not be relieved from segregation by anything he could do within the corporate limits of Detroit, and so he extended his remedy by requiring busing to the suburban communities surrounding Detroit.

Under the trial court's plan, transportation on a vast scale would be required. The court ordered the Detroit Board to acquire at least 295 buses to transport students to 53 outlying school districts. Those suburban districts were not part of the original case, and there was no claim they had committed any constitutional violations. By a 5 to 4 decision, the U.S. Supreme Court held that the trial court exceeded its authority, and restricted its remedy to the City of Detroit only, excluding the suburban school districts. (*Milliken v. Bradley*, (1974) 418 U.S. 717).

De Facto Segregation

"*De facto* segregation" means segregation caused by where people live, without any intent or actions to influence public school enrollment. A black neighborhood would most likely have a black elementary school, a "segregated" school. Some school authorities concluded that the problems were the same in *de facto* segregated schools as in the South where segregation existed by law, and they tried to alleviate the problems of segregation by requiring "racial balance" in the schools.

The New York State Commission of Education in 1963 directed each school system to develop a plan reducing enrollment of minority students to 50 percent. The courts, however, overruled the Commission, stating that while the constitution forbids segregation by law, it does not, however, prohibit racial imbalance; nor does it mandate racial balance. (*Hummel v. Allen*, (1963) 245 N.Y.S. 2d 876). Other courts refused to adopt an "affirmative" policy, without fault, of balancing the races. (*Deal v. Cincinnati Board of Education*, (1964) 369 F. 2d 55, *Downs v. Board of Education of Kansas City*, (1964) 336 F. 2d 988, *Bell v. School City of Gary*, (1964) 324 Fed. 209).

California, on the other hand, adopted a policy of eliminating segregation regardless of its cause.

In 1962 the California State Board of Education took its first step toward eliminating school segregation. The State Board required local school authorities to "exert all effort to avoid and eliminate segregation of children on account of race or color." Riverside responded by amending the policy on boundaries to permit "ethnic composition of the residents near the school, the student body, and the adjacent schools and school areas" to be considered for the purpose of avoiding *de facto* segregation. Some boundary changes were made in both the elementary and secondary schools. The "Lowell School Policy" of Open Enrollment was expanded to the Irving and Casa Blanca schools. All grades were open to such policy instead of being limited to fifth and sixth grades, "consistent with the goal of ultimately integrating the three schools [Lowell, Irving, and Casa Blanca]. "

In 1963 the California Supreme Court dealt with gerrymandering by the Pasadena School Board for the purpose of creating segregation. (*Jackson v. Pasadena City School District*, (1963) 59 Cal. 2d 876). Although the case was about deliberate segregation, the Court announced a strong policy against school segregation whatever the cause:

> So long as large numbers of Negroes live in segregated areas, school authorities will be confronted with difficult problems in providing Negro children with the kind of education they are entitled to have. Residential segregation is in itself an evil which tends to frustrate the youth in the area and to cause antisocial attitudes and behavior.

> Where such segregation exists it is not enough for a school board to refrain from affirmative discriminatory conduct. The harmful influence on the children will be reflected and intensified in the classroom if school attendance is determined on a geographic basis without corrective measures. The right to an equal opportunity for education and the harmful consequences of segregation require that school boards take steps, insofar as reasonably feasible, to alleviate racial imbalance in schools *regardless of its cause* [italics added].

In the Jackson case policy, school boards were given wide discretion. The definition of "reasonably feasible," to which the policy applied, was:

> School authorities, of course, are not required to attain an exact apportionment of Negroes among the schools, and consideration must be given to the various factors in each case, including the practical necessities of governmental operation. For example, consideration should be given, on the one hand, to the degree of racial imbalance in the particular school and the extent to which it affects the opportunity for education and, on the other hand, to such matters as the difficulty and effectiveness of revising school boundaries so as to eliminate segregation and the availability of other facilities to which students can be transferred.

The Riverside School Board was well aware of the Jackson case. I read it to them at an open meeting. Against this background, the Board faced the confrontation in 1965.

Other Types of Discrimination

The Rosa Parks Story

In the latter part of the 1950s and the early part of the 1960s, there were discrimination battles going on outside of education. The Rosa Parks story is one of the important symbols of the Civil Rights Movement. The U.S. Congress called Rosa Parks "the first lady of civil rights" and in 1979 she was awarded the Presidential Medal of Freedom. A posthumous statue of her was placed in the United States Capitol's National Statuary Hall.

Rosa Parks was a well-respected African-American, a 42-year-old woman, married, and living in Montgomery, Alabama. She was active in the Montgomery chapter of the NAACP. She had a good job as a seamstress in a local department store. One day in December 1955, after working all day long, she boarded a bus for home, just as she had done countless times before. She sat in an empty seat in the first row of back seats reserved for blacks in the "colored" section. There were 10 seats ahead of her reserved for white passengers. The sections were not fixed but were determined by a moveable sign. When the bus driver noticed that the white section had been filled up and several white passengers were standing, he moved the "colored" sign behind Parks and demanded that Parks and three other blacks give up their seats. The other three blacks complied. Parks quietly and courageously refused.

The bus driver summoned the police and they arrested Rosa Parks and took her away. She was charged with disorderly conduct and violating the laws of local segregation known as "Jim Crow laws." She was fined $10 plus $4 in court costs. Her arrest sparked a yearlong boycott of the Montgomery bus system in which blacks comprised more than 75 percent of the ridership. The segregation law was repealed following the federal court ruling in *Browder v. Gayle*, 142 F. Supp. 707.

Sit-ins

The next target of the Civil Rights Movement was the segregated lunch counter. Blacks could purchase merchandise from a store, but couldn't eat at the store's lunch counter. On February 1, 1960, four freshmen from the all-black North Carolina Agricultural and Technical College walked into the local F. W. Woolworth Company store in Greensboro, N.C. They purchased some school supplies, and then took whites-only seats at the store's lunch counter and requested service. They were denied service but they sat there quietly until the store closed. The next day some twenty black students took lunch-counter seats, and the wire services picked up the story. Over the next two months, sit-ins spread to more than 50 cities.

Students had some "Do's and Don'ts":

> Don't strike back or curse back if abused.
> Don't block entrances to the stores and aisles.
> Show yourself friendly and courteous at all times.
> Sit straight and always face the counter.
> Remember the teachings of Jesus Christ, Mohammad, Gandhi,
> and Martin Luther King.
> Remember love and nonviolence.
> May God bless each of you.

Typically a lunch counter would close when a sit-in began. But when the students were attacked, police began to arrest those participating in the sit-ins. The charge was usually disorderly conduct, and when convicted, jail time or a fine was the result. They generally chose to serve jail time rather than pay a fine. By August 1961 over 3,000 arrests were made. The Civil Rights Act of 1964 declared segregation in all public accomodation unlawful.

Freedom Rides

CORE (Congress on Racial Equality) organized the first Freedom Ride in May 1961 on Greyhound and Trailways buses. The plan was to ride from Washington, D.C., to New Orleans challenging segregated seating on buses and segregated waiting rooms at interstate bus stops. The Freedom Rides included black and white activists. In Anniston, Alabama, one bus was firebombed and burned. In Birmingham, a mob of Ku Klux Klan mercilessly beat the Riders with baseball bats, iron pipes, and bicycle chains. A white mob again beat Riders arriving in Montgomery. With the injured Riders still in the hospital, replacement Riders continued to ride to Jackson, Mississippi. There they were immediately arrested when they tried to use the "whites only" facilities at the depot. During the summer months of 1961, more than 60 different Freedom Rides crossed the South. Many of them included Jackson, Mississippi, where every Rider was arrested—more than 300 in all. In December 1961, the Interstate Commerce Commission ruled segregation on public transportation illegal.

The Birmingham Bombing

In 1963, after months of protests and marches by Dr. King and attacks by police on non-violent protestors, Birmingham, Alabama, business leaders reached an agreement with the Southern Christian Leadership Conference to integrate public facilities in the city. Not everyone agreed with ending racial segregation. In the early Sunday morning of September 15, 1963 a box of dynamite with a time delay was placed under the steps of the 16th Street Baptist Church near the basement. The church had been a rallying point for Civil Rights activists during the spring of 1963.

Left: 101st Airborne Division escort the Little Rock Nine students into Central High School.

Below: Rosa Parks and Dr. Martin Luther King, Jr., ca. 1955.

Above top: Alabama officers await demonstrators at the Edmund Pettis Bridge.

Above middle: Greensboro protesters Ronald Martin, Robert Patterson, and Mark Martin at the F.W. Woolworth lunch counter in 1960.

Above bottom: Freedom Riders firebombed in Anniston, Alabama.

Martin Luther King, Jr., and Ralph David Abernathy frequently used the church as a meeting place.

That Sunday morning, 26 children were walking into the basement assembly room of the church when the bomb exploded. Four young girls, aged 11 to 14, were killed and 22 were injured. As the story reached the national and international press it became one of the turning points of the Civil Rights Movement. Dr. King wired Governor George Wallace: "The blood of four little children . . . is on your hands. Your irresponsible and misguided actions have crested in Birmingham and Alabama—the atmosphere that induced continued violence and murder."

A witness identified Robert Chambliss, a KKK member, as the man who placed the bomb. He was arrested but only charged with possessing 122 sticks of dynamite without a permit. Three weeks later, after the bombing, he was convicted with a fine of $100 and a six-month jail sentence. Years later, in 1971, when the FBI files were opened, he was charged with murder, found guilty, and sentenced to life imprisonment. He died in prison.

The Selma March

The political and emotional peak of the Civil Rights Movement grew out of white resistance to voting rights in Selma, Alabama. The death of protestor Jimmy Lee Jackson led to plans for a protest march from Selma to Montgomery, the state capital, to demand that the Governor protect voting rights protestors. Governor Wallace denounced the march as a threat to public safety and declared he would take all measures necessary to prevent the march from happening. The marchers left out of Brown Chapel on March 7, 1965. On the Pettis Bridge, the marchers were attacked by state and local police with billy clubs and tear gas, leading to the naming of the day as "Bloody Sunday." After a federal court injunction, the Selma to Montgomery march was held, beginning on March 21st, this time protected by 2,000 soldiers of the U.S. Army and 1,900 members of the Alabama National Guard under federal command. Dr. King and Ralph Bunche led the way.

Conclusion

The demonstrations of 1961 through 1965, and the violence of the Los Angeles 1965 Watts riots, surely had an effect on Riverside as we faced the school crisis of September 1965—the burning of Lowell School, followed by a school boycott led by black leaders, and the demand for immediate integration.

The following remarks were taken from an interview with Ray Berry in *Path to Understanding, 1989,* a video production of the Riverside Unified School District.

The immediate catalysts were the fact that minority people in the nation, particularly in California and particularly in the metropolitan area of Los Angeles, were being freed to speak up, be seen, to have their say. The Watts riots in Los Angeles I think brought that to a peak, so that suddenly, almost overnight in effect, it became—maybe not all right—but at least people could dare to say, "Hey, we don't like this anymore. We want our schools to be better, or we want out of here, we want those good schools for our kids."

What do you do for a child that isn't doing well? How do you compensate for poverty, how do you compensate for bigotry and prejudice and all those kinds of awful things?

We tried a lot of . . . efforts, small types, better programs, smaller class size, a change in teachers, library in the school, a number of things. We had a lot of hopes for them. We, being I, plus the parents, plus the teachers and the principals that worked on it. But we saw no real change.

And we began to realize after awhile, that in spite of our hopes, that we were really looking at generations of impact of prejudice and bigotry, and to think of changing that overnight with a few relatively simple adjustments just wasn't going to work.

RAY BERRY
ASSOCIATE SUPERINTENDENT

Emmett Raymond "Ray" Berry, Jr. came to Riverside as the personnel director for the Riverside Unified School District after having served as a superintendent in Carpinteria.

He was promoted to assistant superintendent in 1961, and associate superintendent from 1962 to 1968. In 1968, he became superintendent, succeeding Bruce Miller.

In addition to leading the staff effort to integrate Riverside schools, Berry is also noted for his theories and implementation of decentralized decision-making and the related restructuring of school district administration.

Following his retirement in 1978, he joined the education faculty at the University of California, Riverside. He eventually retired to Cambria.

Left to right: Alice Key, Robert Bland, Etienne Caroline.

CHAPTER 4 – BACKGROUND FOR INTEGRATION

Summer of 1963

Late in the summer of 1963 I had a visit from Jesse Wall, a young black teacher at Ramona High School. He came to my office at the law firm of Best Best & Krieger at 12th and Orange Streets. I didn't know him personally but I knew something about him: he was a teacher in our system at Ramona High School, he was the president of the NAACP, and he had just received the "Man of the Year" award from the Junior Chamber of Commerce. Since I had received the same award earlier, I was tuned in to other winners.

His visit wasn't legal, it was school-related. He was trying to form a Human Relations Council for Riverside. He thought there were some racial problems in the community and the best way to address them was through this Council. He had been talking to city councilmen and other community leaders, and he had not received much support from them. He wanted to know whether the School District and I would endorse such a formation, and would we be able to participate in it. I told him "Yes. By all means." It surprised him. Apparently I was the only person at that point who had simply said, "Yes."[10]

That reply got us off to a good start.

---

10.   The Human Relations Council was eventually set up, and Dr. Donald Taylor, assistant superintendent, represented me at most of the meetings.

We had been talking about racial problems in the community. Then I said to him, "Tell me about the school system. How are the minority teachers perceived? Do we have enough of them? Are they doing a good job? Are the minority students treated fairly? How are the minority students performing? Do the minority students feel discriminated against? How do the minority students and the white majority get along?"

This led to a very long conversation, and for the first time I realized there were racial problems in the schools and I had not been aware of them. The message, in a nutshell, was that there was a real need to deal with racial relations.

I told Superintendent of Schools Bruce Miller about my conversation with Wall. My court schedule permitting, I met with Bruce every Monday for lunch at Sage's. Sage's was a great gathering place—a forerunner of the one-stop shop with groceries, bakery, drug store, and a coffee shop that was like a diner in a small town. Sage's was on Magnolia Avenue where the Big Five Sporting goods store is now located.

The School Board met every other Monday at 4 p.m. We reviewed the Board's agenda for the forthcoming meeting. But more importantly, I took the opportunity to find out what was going on in the school district.

Both Mr. Miller and I were aware of the rising racial tensions in the nation and in California. In 1962 the California State Board of Education had adopted a policy of eliminating segregation, whatever its cause. And in August 1963, Martin Luther King, Jr., delivered his "I Have a Dream" speech on the steps of the Lincoln Memorial in Washington, D.C. There were over 250,000 civil rights supporters present as a part of the "March on Washington." The speech was a defining moment of the civil rights movement.

The fight against segregation was no longer a Southern problem. There was growing realization of the problems inherent in any segregated school situation—whatever the cause—an idea that I hadn't understood at first.

We agreed that we needed to get a better understanding of what was going on in the Riverside schools. We talked with the Board, black community leaders, Associate Superintendent Ray Berry, and other administrators, and that led us to the conference at San Dimas.

The San Dimas Conference, 1963

Traditionally, just before the opening of school each fall, all of the principals and the top administrators of the Riverside schools had gathered at the conference center at the Voorhis Campus of Cal Poly San Dimas. This year, Mr. Miller and I decided that the conference was a good opportunity for an exploration of the problems of minority groups in the Riverside schools. It was decided that I would attend, and an invitation would go out to the black community leaders interested in our schools.

I don't remember how the black leaders were chosen, probably by Wall, but in attendance were: Jesse Wall; Mrs. Alice Key, publisher of *The VOICE* (Victory Over Inequities, Civic and Economic), a weekly tabloid newspaper serving the Eastside of Riverside; Robert Bland, who had come directly from the University of Virginia to the Naval Ordnance Lab in Norco, and was education chairman of the NAACP (and later one of the boycott leaders in Riverside); and Etienne Caroline, a Riverside police detective. They told their own personal stories about what it was like to be black in Riverside, and what had happened to them as children. They told us what it was like to be called inferior, no matter what a black person's aspirations or inherent abilities might be. They did not, and could not, share the American dream: if you work hard, the opportunities will be without limit. They did not talk to us in terms of criticism, but rather a plea for help. They foresaw problems for the whole nation if we were not to make progress with race relations. They hoped that we, the leaders of the Riverside school system and the community, would understand the problems and help to solve them. It was a moving experience, and for the first time I began to understand how alienated those in the minority community felt.

My own personal childhood experiences with minorities were limited. I am a first generation American, having parents who emigrated from England after World War I. I was raised in a white, workingman's neighborhood in the southern part of Los Angeles. I went to Washington High School from 1938 to 1941. Washington was located in the outer part of the city, with farms and open space on both sides of the school and extending all the way to the ocean. Minorities in my high school were not blacks or Mexican Americans but a few Japanese-American students who came from the nearby truck farms. The students themselves were not discriminated against in school. They were in the school's social and honors organizations and one was our football quarterback. But in 1942, students of Japanese ancestry no longer attended our school. Because of World War II, they and their families, like all Japanese who were living in the Western states, were interned in camps in various parts of the country.

The African Americans in my high school days lived primarily in Watts. Their high school was Jefferson, an all black school. Washington and Jefferson were teamed in the same division for athletics: football, basketball, track, baseball. The teams would play alternately at each other's schools. I can remember being bused over to Jefferson for football games. Safety was never an issue, but neither was there interaction between the two student bodies, except to yell at the direction of the cheerleaders. I was on the track team and we had an excellent relay team. I ran the third leg, 220 yards. But we lost to Jefferson in our dual meet, came in second to Jefferson in the quarterfinal meet, and in the final all-city meet also came in second to Jefferson. The all-city meet was held in the Los Angeles Coliseum before 30,000 people. Jefferson broke the California record; we did too. However, there is no recognition for coming in second.

In all these races I never talked with the students from Jefferson as friends. They didn't talk with me either. It was just the way things were.

There were plenty of black athletes that I rooted for—Jesse Owens, Joe Lewis, Kenny Washington (the UCLA quarterback), and Jackie Robinson, also from UCLA. But in my childhood days I was unaware of the discrimination and frustration they must have suffered in their private lives.

After the San Dimas Conference presentation by the black leaders, the meeting was thrown open to a general discussion. There were lots of questions and some pretty basic candid discussions. Not everyone was in agreement that the minority groups had not been well treated. Some felt that the plight of the blacks was their own fault. But the overwhelming sentiment to come out of that meeting was that we should do something more than we had been doing and recognize the problems of minorities in a special way. This was not unusual for the Riverside school system. We had developed curricula for the gifted since Sputnik and long since had developed programs for persons with disabilities, athletes, and the arts.

Compensatory Education

I reported the results of the San Dimas Conference to the full School Board, and B. Rae Sharp and I were appointed to meet the minority leaders and the administration to develop a policy recognizing the special problems of minority students. We met with the group of leaders who were invited to San Dimas as well as with others.

We had initial disagreements over what the minority schools were like. The minority community was convinced that their schools got poorer teachers, got fewer books, got old furniture, and got second-rate everything. None of this was true. As to the teachers, using Lowell as an example, several of the teachers held master's degrees, two were bilingual, one spoke three languages, two were considered district-wide experts in reading, one was a speech therapist, and the entire staff was well above average in competence. Minorities and the majority were treated alike, but I was realizing that that wasn't enough. We needed to address the *perception* of unequal treatment, reinforced because the special needs of minorities were unmet.

Mr. Bland, the NAACP education chair, had access to school records that showed that minorities placed in the lowest one-third of academic achievement. The schools, he claimed, had done little to correct this gap; the counseling was inadequate; and more minority teachers were needed.

The particular solutions that the minority leaders advanced all turned on improving the education of children at the schools they attended. Integration was rejected in favor of neighborhood schools. At that point, they felt that busing was not an answer and that to move children out of their own schools was only going to compound the problems.

After meeting with the minority community, administration, and teachers, Associate Superintendent Ray Berry developed a program for Compensatory Education which he called "Proposals for Integration." The program was presented to the School Board on October 7, 1963, and encompassed minorities not only at Irving, Lowell, and Casa Blanca, but also students at Liberty, Longfellow, and the junior high schools. It called for providing all elementary schools with libraries, with a top priority going to Lowell and Irving. Teacher aides from the University of California, Riverside (UCR) teaching preparation program were organized, and 21 teaching assistants were placed at Casa Blanca, Irving, and Lowell immediately in October. Black history classes were accelerated. Field trips called "Higher Horizons" were established. Finally, the schools could work directly with organized community groups to adjust attendance boundaries, improve counseling, and promote "greater elementary level integration on both a short- and long-range basis." The School Board unanimously approved the program, to be "implemented immediately."

Many good people were trying to make the program work. They were creative, flexible, and given a free hand—free of bureaucracy and red tape. For example, I was in the desert on legal business when I ran into Dick Purviance who was attending a conference. Somehow we learned that Ralph Bunche, an African American who was the U.S. delegate to the United Nations, would be talking at the Claremont Colleges the next day. Bunche was probably the most famous black man in the nation having won the Nobel Peace Prize in 1950. We agreed that we ought to do something.

Purviance made a few telephone calls to Riverside, and the next day we had a bus loaded with children from Irving and Lowell schools bound for Claremont. There wasn't enough time for the usual parent consent forms, and I don't know how they got the bus in time, or how they found the funds to pay for it, but the students got to go to Claremont. However on arriving, the group discovered that the speech was sold out. Unwilling to take "no" for an answer, Alice Key, the person in charge, sought out Mr. Bunche backstage after his speech, explained that she had a bus load of minority children anxious to see him, and he said, "Well, bring them back." He then spent an hour or so talking with them, which was much more rewarding than the speech ever would have been.

During 1964, other improvements to the programs were instituted. More than 100 voluntary tutors from UCR were assigned to aid children with particular learning problems. The district put a half-time reading teacher at each of the schools with large minority populations. In-service teacher training on racial relations was implemented. A self-help program for parents entitled "Help Your Child at School" was held on four successive Sundays in January and February at the Community Settlement House on the Eastside. More minority teachers were hired. The Open

ESTHER [VELEZ] ANDREWS

LOWELL KINDERGARTEN TEACHER

Esther taught kindergarten at Lowell School starting in 1961. Her classroom, the bungalow building, was later converted to St. James Church of God in Christ when the school site was sold after the fire.

She graduated from Atlantic Union College in Massachusetts, a sister college to La Sierra University. She already had a teaching contract in New York City when she came to visit her brother in Riverside and he encouraged her to stay.

At Lowell, she made lifelong friendships with fellow teachers Horace Jackson [Riverside's first black middle and high school principal], Doris [Doskocil] Haddy, and Barbara [Wheelock] Hamilton.

This interview focuses on Esther's teaching experience at Lowell. She also served as an administrator for the integration effort. She shares an experience in that role on page 103.

Esther [Velez] Andrews: *I told my brother, if they hire me on the spot, I'll stay. . . . I was sitting in the lobby and Ray Berry comes by. He looks at me and he tells his personnel officer, "Bring her in to see me," and an hour later I was hired.*

He had in mind to put me at Lowell because it was a school that was in transition, going through all kinds of problems. He also hired Horace Jackson at the same time. And we went to Lowell.

When I got there, it was already going through the transition of becoming segregated. There were a few Anglo families, but it was primarily Mexican and majority black.

We had a staff that was so close. It was like a family. It was my best experience, being accepted and teamed. It was progressive, we had teachers with master's degrees at that time. I studied abroad. In fact, in one of the articles in the paper, Dick Purviance, the principal, explains our backgrounds [Daily Enterprise, September 1965]. Because the gossip was that the teachers were incompetent, they weren't trained, they would only [be at Lowell or Irving Schools] because they couldn't go anywhere else. Dick Purviance really tells how competent we were. What we brought to the school. We were very progressive. Doris was an excellent reading teacher. We all had specialties, we all had something to give that he could really boast about.

Ray Berry brought what was called Compensatory Education to the school, but that didn't satisfy the parents. I had kindergarten, so what Compensatory Education brought [to my classroom] was more money for arts and music, more books. The base of it was to enrich the school, give it a head start, compared to other schools. The benefits were really in the upper grades, one through six. But I didn't get any relief from teaching 60 kids a day [30 children in each of the morning and afternoon kindergarten].

In the beginning, it was parents and administration. When the parents began to balk against Compensatory Education, then the staff started to [be involved at the invitation of] Ray Berry, because he believed in staff participation, he was marvelous at really including us. That's when I became aware of the discontent, the way the thinking was going at the time. We used to meet at Lowell, and we used to meet in the lunchroom-staff room. It could have been about a year and a half before the school was firebombed.

These were prominent black people who were trying to make a change, make that change happen. They were all aspiring professionals. I remember Donald Renfro and Robert Bland. They wanted equal education and they wanted the best for their children. They wanted them in the real world, what they considered the real world. They wanted their children to be exposed to all the opportunities that were out there for whites. They felt that at Lowell, the children wouldn't have that opportunity.

I spent many nights in meetings with them, ten or eleven o'clock at night at Lowell in my bungalow with Renfro and Bland, and many other parents. They really had quite a large committee of black parents.

. . . Andrews continued on page 35

Enrollment policy was opened wide to include all grades at the three *de facto* segregated schools. In addition Mr. Purviance —one of our most distinguished principals, originally at Lowell and then promoted to North High School—and Jesse Wall were put in charge of the Compensatory Education Program, under the supervision of Ray Berry.

The 1964 school year had been a good one in Riverside insofar as racial relations were concerned. Early on, I met with a group of thirteen black and Mexican-American leaders to discuss and make improvements to the Compensatory Education Program. Those in attendance from the minority community included: Jess Ybarra, Gay Caroline, Etienne Caroline, Jesse Carlos, Robert Bland, Bill Davis, Jack Clarke, Sr., Alice Key, Mrs. Frances Allen, J. Baker, and Donald Renfro (who later, in 1965, presented the petition to close both Irving and Lowell schools). Among those attending from the school administration were James Jordon and Jesse Wall.

Some of the 1964 improvements mentioned above were the result of this meeting, but the attitude toward integration was changing. The minority representatives wanted to continue the Compensatory Education Program, but they also wanted to work on the problems of *de facto* segregation and not let the program be a substitute for real integration. Remarkably, they suggested we aim toward closing Casa Blanca and placing the students in adjacent schools.

In May 1964, the Riverside Board of Education received an award from the NAACP for "outstanding service to the community in acknowledgement of and sincere efforts toward resolution of the problem of *de facto* segregation in Riverside."

One year later, however, in May 1965, I heard the rumblings of discontent over the Compensatory Education Program. Etienne Caroline asked me if we could have lunch at the Squire restaurant near UCR. He told me of the general dissatisfaction with the program. The Board had given these people a free hand, but the administration was "muffing the ball." He was particularly critical of Jesse Wall. He said everybody had understood that class sizes would be reduced, but that had not been done. People thought improvement was moving too slowly. I discussed the conversation in detail with Ray Berry, and he indicated that Jesse Wall and Dick Purviance did not get along as well as had been expected, which led to some failures in the program. He felt that at the start of the school year in the fall we would have to make some changes. As to the class size issue, the budget for the 1965 school year already included substantial reductions in class sizes. In all, the problems in the program could probably be fixed. But Berry, in a report to the Board in the summer of 1965, took a longer-range view:

Left to right: Bruce Miller, Arthur Littleworth, B. Rae Sharp.

Above: Gay Caroline, the 1964 president of the Riverside chapter of the NAACP.

The following is excerpted from an article she wrote about her trip to the NAACP national convention: "We Have So Much To Do," The VOICE, July 16, 1964.

"We were reminded that desegregation is an integral part of good education, that compensatory education and integrated education are needed simultaneously. We must look closely at special programs, i.e., higher horizons, etc. and reject them when they are used as a substitute for desegregation, or are misused to perpetuate the same old doctrine of separate but equal. Compensatory education and integrated education should go hand in hand, but if we are forced to make a choice, then we must choose integration."

Andrews continued from page 33

I shared with them that I understood the need to be exposed to what was out there, what their children were going to face. I always felt that children needed to have the opportunity to understand what they were competing against. But I strongly argued with them many, many nights about the education they were getting at our school. In the end both of them agreed, and said that yes, the education was good but that the exposure they wanted for their children was not there.

I don't think Renfro and Bland were thinking of any destruction. They just wanted the district to act. I think what happened as the talks went on, they realized what they wanted. They realized that they needed to have a decision for their children before it was too late.

At the end of meetings, we'd have a follow up discussion. Ray kept telling us, "We need to look for other avenues." He wasn't really mentioning desegregation or closing the school or anything like that but he was looking to us to bring in other ways we could either enrich the school or make some decisions. I could feel that in him as we talked and we realized what was happening. Even Dick Purviance realized that, too. He was a smart man. They could see that [Bland and Renfro] were not going to be comfortable or accepting of what the district was offering. Especially, these two gentlemen. They were bright, they were really bright people.

I think it was a process with the discussions. They would say to us, "No, I don't think that Compensatory Education is the answer to what we want." We started hearing that and we started to hear that they wanted their children to experience the world the way they experienced it. I think they were referring to their experience going to college, their experience getting degrees. The pain they went through in that effort, they didn't want their children to go through that. They wanted them to have access to dealing in the real world, because the real world was majority white.

That's what I think they were saying, they wanted integration, but I am not sure they understood it themselves. I think it was a process that we were going through in the discussions of "What is Compensatory Education? What would it lead to?" And I think the outcome was not what they wanted, the outcome of Compensatory Education alone. I feel very strongly that they wanted integration from the outset but that they did not know how to say that or express that.

Considerable thought and effort should continue to be found, not only on how to improve programs in *de facto* segregated schools, but *how to eliminate the schools themselves* [italics added].

The problems of the minorities were those that had been recognized all along: high drop-out rates, discrimination, home conditions that limited children's success in school, and insufficient incentives to develop their potential. These were national problems, and it would take time to solve them. (Many say we still haven't made much progress.) In my own mind, I knew it was going to take several years to show real educational progress from the Compensatory Education Program. Later, we would learn that the minority community had far different expectations. One of the reasons for the growing support for integration was the perceived failure of the Compensatory Education Program to change student outcomes, after only one and a half years of implementation.

The Compensatory Education Program in Riverside was a small part of the solution, but perhaps its greatest benefit was something intangible—hope. By recognizing the special needs of minorities, and by trying to do something about the problems, the school system established some measure of trust.

This newspaper photo from The Press-Enterprise *shows local children playing on the steps of Lowell School after the fire. Debris from the fire is visible behind the temporary fencing.*

CHAPTER 5 — THE WEEK OF HELL

Tuesday — The Burning of Lowell School

I had spent the Labor Day weekend of 1965 at Balboa Island with my family. I was excited not only about the opening of school, but I had a major zoning case set for Tuesday, September 7, before the Riverside City Council.[11] The first indication that something was wrong was when I came into my office at 8:30 a.m. on Tuesday and received a telephone call from Mayor Ben Lewis. He told me that he had been invited to a meeting the Friday before the holiday and that he didn't know too much about the purpose, but he attended anyway. It was in one of the homes in the Eastside. The gist of the meeting was that the people were very dissatisfied with the schools transfer policy, the Open Enrollment policy, and they felt there had been discrimination in its administration.

11. The issue was the city's first large shopping center. I represented the firm that had the Bullock's department store as the major tenant. The shopping center was to be built on the site of California Baptist College. This was before the present day expansion of the college. At the time, the college was to have a new campus somewhere in Riverside. The opposition was Broadway-May Company at Tyler, the present day site of the Galleria. There could be only one approved location.

We had a School Board meeting scheduled for that afternoon at 4 p.m. The mayor suggested that we would probably receive a delegation at the meeting. The group he met with was angry and not too well informed. The Watts Riots had ended only 20 days earlier in Los Angeles, and at the meeting they suggested that if they did not get what they wanted it might be "Burn, Baby, Burn" in Riverside as well. He wanted me to be aware of this, and would I please keep him informed.

Since the case I had before the city council was to have an enormous impact on the city of Riverside, I didn't have much time to do anything about the mayor's call, except I felt that later I would talk to Mr. Miller about it. I went to Riverside City Hall at nine o'clock for the hearing in the case, but because of the large crowd the hearing was moved to the auditorium of Lincoln School.[12] Prior to the beginning of the hearing the city manager told me that he had just been informed by the fire department that Lowell School had been burned down. I wondered if this is what the mayor had been telling me about? I wondered if there would be more fires? It was hard to keep my mind on my work. I was tempted to ask for a continuance of the hearing, but I did not know if the cause of the fire was arson or not. So I announced to the city council that I just learned of the fire at Lowell School, and that I would make my presentation and leave as soon as possible. But as a practical matter there was no way to get away until about 12:30 p.m. So I left the hearing and went directly to the school administration office.

I found that the school administrators, Mr. Bruce Miller and Mr. Richard Purviance (the principal at Lowell), had been at Lowell School most of the morning, trying to save some of the records and some of the library books, and also answering questions from the fire department. It was early afternoon before I was able to speak with Mr. Miller. He told me that he understood that the fire had started sometime in the early morning hours, and that the fire marshal indicated that it looked like arson. I told him about the call I had received from the mayor, and I believe that at this time Mr. Miller knew about a petition that had been circulated, and that there was to be some kind of delegation at the Board meeting.

The fire department and the police department arrived and questioned us at length. The fire marshal confirmed that the fire was arson. The fire apparently started at about 2:00 a.m., but the fire department was not called until around 4:00 a.m.

At 4:00 p.m. it was time for the School Board meeting. Mr. Miller wanted to know what the Board thought we should do with the children displaced by the fire. I remember saying that I didn't think we should make a decision at this four o'clock meeting; it was too hasty and we needed time to think things through.

12. Lincoln School was the first school in Riverside. The deed had been signed by John W. North in 1870. The site was between 6th and 7th streets on Lime Street. The school was eventually torn down and replaced with office buildings.

Barbara [Wheelock] Hamilton (BH) and
Doris [Doskocil] Haddy (DH):

BH: When [Lowell, prior to 1961] was integrated, it was probably a third white, a third black, a third Hispanic. And it worked very well. It was good for everybody.

DH: But then after Alcott opened the first year, we had some Anglo students, but I think by the third year, we didn't have maybe but two in the whole school. They just disappeared. So it became just Hispanic and African American.

I can remember parents, particularly parents from the South that had moved to Riverside, coming down and asking about the textbooks, asking did we have the same textbooks as the other schools in the city? And I said, "Yes, we do. You move to another [school], it's the same textbooks." They wanted to see them. They were coming from the South, and for me it was, "Why are they asking these questions?" I'd always lived in California, so why would I assume anything else? Well then, in talking, segregated schools in the South had old textbooks, not the new ones. They were not getting the same supplies as other schools.

BH: [On the day of the fire] the secretary called us and said the school burned down.

DH: We thought she was joking. I didn't believe it. "You're to stay home." She started getting serious and it was, "Whoa, what's happening here?" . . . One of the teachers, Liz Gillette, lived on Ivy Street. It was decided that we would meet there in the afternoon about one o'clock. . . . We were all in shock. . . . They said a Molotov cocktail, whatever that was . . .

BH: That was the word at the time, so who knows?

DH: The inside of the school was just covered with black oil . . . soot, and then the burned part was partitioned off and you couldn't go into that. The rest of it was all intact. I remember the library had helpers there cleaning the books, because the books had all the soot and oil, the residue from the fire.

BH: I was going to move to the room where they threw [the incendiary device] in. . . . So I couldn't get any of my things, I think I could go in and look at my desk at one point, but it was pretty much of a mess.

BH: I think it was a huge, huge shock. Never, ever, would we have imagined, that this would have happened.

DH: We had such a wonderful staff and we loved the kids.

BH: It was out of the blue. Even with everything that had gone on in Los Angeles, and the whole business. . . . I would never have expected anybody [to burn the school].

DH: There were two wings outside; one of those was moved to Alcott a few years later. It is still there.

BH: That's where we taught, in those wings outside, after. . . . When this happened, the students had a choice of staying or going. They did not have to stay at Lowell School. The teachers had a choice also. Some teachers

DORIS [DOSKOCIL] HADDY AND BARBARA [WHEELOCK] HAMILTON

TEACHERS AT LOWELL SCHOOL

Doris [Doskocil] Haddy and Barbara [Wheelock] Hamilton were young teachers at Lowell School for several years before it was burned on September 7, 1965. Barbara taught grades four, five, and six. Doris taught grades three and four.

When Lowell School closed in 1966, Barbara left teaching, transferring with her military husband to South Dakota. Doris stayed at Lowell as a reading specialist until it closed, then went to Emerson School, and later to teach at several other Riverside schools, ending her career at Liberty School.

Today, Barbara is back in Riverside, and she, Doris, and Esther [Velez] Andrews, a core group of Lowell teachers, are reunited.

. . . Hamilton and Haddy continued on page 41

Tuesday —
The Board Meeting: The Call for the Closing of Lowell and Irving Schools

The School Board meeting started promptly at 4:00 p.m. The boardroom was filled with African Americans, and it was standing room only. People were outside as well. Tension filled the room, but people were orderly. The Board and the administration did not know what prompted this large turnout. I dispensed with the routine agenda and got to what I thought the audience wanted—information about the Lowell fire. Instead, the Board was presented with a surprise petition by a Mr. Donald Renfro,[13] PTA president at Lowell and the spokesperson for the dissatisfied group.

The substance of the petition was that Lowell and Irving Schools should be closed, apparently as soon as possible. The petition had been circulated over the Labor Day weekend, and they had been able to pick up about 400 signatures in a couple of days. A discussion between the Board and the audience ensued revealing that the community group had indeed held a meeting on Friday with the mayor. Why they did not invite any school representatives was never made clear. The principal subject for their Friday meeting was that the Open Enrollment policy had been improperly administered and that, in fact, it didn't exist at all.

The transfer policy stated that if you wanted to move to a new school you had to apply and wait until there was an opening at that school. If the school you wanted had room for more students, the applying student simply had to enroll there. Some schools, like Alcott, were quite crowded, and an applying student had to wait for an opening in the student's grade level.

Apparently the impetus of the petition drive was Mrs. Donald Renfro's application under the Open Enrollment policy to transfer her children out of Lowell. Although her application was filed weeks before school started in the fall, the application met resistance and delay. Her husband, who was the PTA president at Lowell, decided to check this out himself. In his opinion, he found that the administration was uncooperative. This was the issue that prompted the claim of discrimination within the administration, or that the policy wasn't being implemented at all. There was a fair amount of discussion on this topic, with the audience telling of their experiences. I tried to explain the policy and assure the group that the administration would follow through with an investigation of their complaints.

There was no mention of the burning of Lowell School during the first part of the meeting.

During the discussion on the petition it became apparent that there was a great deal of dissatisfaction—contempt really—for the Compensatory Education Program.

13. Don Renfro worked as a manager for IBM. Later, when an article about my retirement from the School Board came out in the January 13, 1973 issue of *The Press-Enterprise*, he had moved to the Oakland area and was quoted: "Littleworth is quite a guy. He stayed calm through the whole thing."

Hamilton and Haddy continued from page 39

chose to go and some, that had been teaching a lower grade, chose to stay and teach an upper grade. All the lower grades had to [transfer], up to third grade. Four, five, and six had a choice.

DH: They could go to any school in town, or they could stay.

BH: Lots of parents came and talked to us, should they go or should they stay? One of the reasons, I remember, for saying that I think your child should stay, was that I was going to have a combination [a class with two grades together], so I had [only] 19 students. How often is that going to happen?

DH: Before the fire I had 39 kids. . . . But the parents were very supportive, almost all of them came to parent conferences. We had really, out of the big class that I had, maybe two that didn't come. And if they didn't come, we went to their house. . . . I remember the first day we went back on the job after the fire, there were policemen everywhere.

BH: We also had backup plain-clothes detectives; we met at Liz's and drove to school and the detectives took us in, but nothing happened, it was fine.

DH: I remember Pat [Kennington] Cowan and I rode together, and we parked a little ways from the school and we got out and walked, and there were people boycotting the school, and they stopped and said, "Are you teachers?" We knew right away they didn't belong in the community because we knew everyone in the community. They would have known us. We said, "Yes we are," and then they let us pass. They were trying to stop the parents from coming to school.

Left to right: 2009 Lowell School reunion. Don Miller, custodian; teachers: Doris [Doskocil] Haddy, Henry Blanco, Barbara [Wheelock] Hamilton, Esther [Velez] Andrews, Edna Waugh, and Horace Jackson.

BH: The other interesting thing is that several parents whose children were going to the Freedom School came and . . . they felt they didn't have a choice because of their peers in the community, they would have had a problem. But it worked both ways. Some of them felt it was very important to [go to the Freedom School], and some, they didn't want to do it.

DH: But I remember that first day . . . they told us to stay in the rooms. . . . I wasn't afraid. . . . except seeing those guys [the plainclothes police] out there, sort of made you afraid. . . . One classroom of kids showed up, 30 to 35. . . . The parents were scared, like the rest of us. It was a scary, scary day . . . and I remember I was so glad the day was over, because you just felt emotionally drained. You knew that all this change was happening, and it wasn't going to take time, it was now. It's here!

[You thought], "What's going to happen tomorrow?" . . . Every day, something different was happening, and you just had to roll with it.

There was a sense of loss. I helped put the kids on the bus the first day they integrated [kindergarten through third grade]. It was a sense of loss to see your kids going somewhere else. I mean, they were our kids. And then when the school finally closed . . . that was when it hit us . . . that was sad. You didn't really want to go to another school. Because your feelings about this school, and the staff, you'd been there five years. It was a wonderful experience. It was a great school.

41

Speakers felt that it had not been working fast enough, that it wasn't appropriate for the times. Many people in the group became hostile and berated us because we had not, as they put it, complied with the Supreme Court Decision of 1954.[14] There was a great deal of criticism of the School Board and administration for not having done anything for the minority problem—specifically for not having integrated all of the schools some time earlier.

Mayor Ben Lewis.

The group grew angrier and more rude. For some relief, I asked Mayor Ben Lewis and Riverside City Councilman John Sotelo if they would like to say anything. It was a mistake to call upon the mayor. Mayor Lewis discussed the Friday night meeting he had attended and commented that he didn't think that the way minority grievances had been handled in the riots in Watts was the way to handle them in Riverside. He reported that the group at the meeting said that if they didn't get what they wanted, "It's going to be 'Burn, Baby, Burn' in Riverside." This created a storm of protest, shouting, yelling, and catcalls from the audience. It nearly broke up the meeting.

I was finally able to get the meeting under control. Some audience members denied that this was said, some people tried to explain it, and others said that the mayor had misunderstood. The mayor stoutly denied any misunderstanding, reasserting that he had repeated precisely what was said. This created more angry response, and I felt it was time to move on.

I called on Councilman John Sotelo to speak, relying on him to change the subject from the Friday meeting. I had known him since our days in the Junior Chamber of Commerce and he was a good friend. He was a Mexican American from the Eastside, and he operated a Shell gas station across the street from Irving School. He was respected by both minority and majority communities. He made an appeal on behalf of the people in the audience, asking that they be excused for their manners and for their methods of presentation. He tried to point out that these were very deep feelings and that things had been smoldering for many years, lifetimes in some instances. Basically their intentions were good. He acknowledged that the goals of the minority community had changed. He remembered when they wanted Irving School rebuilt in the 1950s, and that he had been one of the people who had fought the hardest to get Irving rebuilt. He acknowledged that this had been a mistake. He also knew that the

14. In 1954 the Supreme Court ruled that deliberate segregation in the public schools was unconstitutional. The "*de facto*" segregation, caused by residential housing, was not part of that case. This was hardly the right meeting to explain the legal distinction between "*de facto*" segregation and the result of laws requiring or permitting segregation, "*de jure*" segregation.

Ward 2 Councilman John Sotelo.

Compensatory Education Program had been developed based on the leadership of the community, but he felt that times were changing and that we should try to look at the problems as they existed now.

Except for the outburst after the mayor's remarks, the meeting, while not pleasant, had been relatively under control. Finally someone asked what was going to happen to the students of Lowell School. We said that we didn't know; that the fire had happened today, and that we simply had had no chance to make an intelligent policy. We would try to make a decision as quickly as possible.

There was a good deal of pressure on the Board to make a decision on the petition right then and there. I stated, and the other Board members agreed, that we were not about to decide on a petition of that importance with as little information as we had. I wanted to find out more about the Compensatory Education Program and whether or not it was really as deficient as they were saying. I also wanted to investigate the complaints about our Open Enrollment policy. I wanted to know how representative of the entire minority community this audience's views were. I wondered why they had not included Casa Blanca School in this petition. Anything that satisfied the petition might have to include Casa Blanca as well, it seemed. I suggested that we meet with a committee of the group to discuss the petition, as well as the future of the children who had been displaced by the fire. Mr. Renfro, supported by others who were shouting from the audience, said that they didn't want any more talking or more meetings. They wanted action.

I had learned that we must not promise anything that we couldn't deliver. It was probably better to take the wrath of the moment than not be able to fulfill a promise. There had, from the point of view of the minority community, already been too many broken promises.

As a part of his report on Lowell fire, Bruce Miller told the Board that Lowell's main building had been destroyed and recommended double sessions on an emergency basis until more permanent arrangements could be made. This report was, including the recommendation for double sessions, the subject of a Board motion and passed.

The crowd started to get unruly again. Mr. Don Renfro, who had been relatively calm in his presentation up until that time, began to get fired up. He began to berate us, telling us that we were "going to keep his children out in the rain," and that "his children were not going stay out in the rain," and so forth. The whole meeting again became confrontational, worked up, with people calling in the background, "Go get him, Don. You tell him, Don."

There was little the Board could do. The leaders began to storm out, with everyone yelling and shouting at us. The meeting was over. At this point there had been no discussion of a boycott. I suggested to Mr. Miller that he should try to make other recommendations to us as quickly as possible on the displaced children. We could have a special Board meeting if necessary to consider it, but that should be the No. 1 priority.

The Board's reaction at that moment was one of disbelief. We couldn't believe that this could be happening in Riverside. We were jolted by the crowd's disappointment in our previous efforts to improve the education of minority children. People had pointed their fingers at us and said, "For once in your life, why don't you just do something right."

Looking back on it now, I can see that the entire situation was considerably more volatile than it had been in 1963 when we established the Compensatory Education Program—the attacks on the Freedom Riders, the arrests in the sit-ins, Bull Connor unleashing attack dogs on the marchers, the Birmingham bombing resulting in the death of four little girls, Bloody Sunday, and the L.A. riots. We learned that the thinking of the leadership in the minority community had changed since our earlier attempts to grapple with the issue of *de facto* segregation. We saw that over the Labor Day weekend, the minority leaders had settled on a different goal: full integration. We had a community problem as well as an education problem.

Wednesday —
What to Do with the Displaced Children

Wednesday we developed a different plan for the care of the Lowell children. Nobody was in favor of just rebuilding Lowell School, and despite Bruce Miller's initial recommendation, nobody thought that holding double sessions at Lowell was a good idea. So the question was how to accommodate these children in the other schools in the District. We began by trying to find out where we had school spaces, and what we could do about bus transportation starting Monday, the first day of school. This was largely done by Don Taylor.

Then Mr. Miller, Mr. Berry, Mr. Taylor, and I considered alternatives. We had already rejected one alternative, moving them into Irving School. It was near Lowell, but most students were African American and one of the objectives of the minorities' petition was to close Irving. But what about moving a class as a unit to a white school like Pachappa? It had room and could accommodate, for example, a Lowell second grade class. This would mean a segregated school within a school, and we could see

Board sets double sessions at Lowell school temporarily

Civil rights leaders deplore school arson

By T. E. FOREMAN

Representatives of Riverside civil rights organizations today reported having no idea who might have started a fire at Lowell School yesterday morning.

They were in general agreement, however, that the fire merely pointed up a longstanding problem which can not be solved by halfway measures and for which easy answers cannot be found.

PERSONS contacted this morning generally declined to speculate on whether the fire was set by adults or juveniles, whether it was the act of an irresponsible individual or of a group.

Many said they were less concerned about who started the fire than about whether there will be an awakening of community leaders to the seriousness of the problem presented by "segregated" schools such as Lowell and Irving.

Alice Key, leader of VOICE (Victory Over Inequities, Civil and Economic), who has worked as a librarian at Lowell School, said, "Any sane, rational person is anti-anarchy and opposed to lawlessness. It's stupefying for a school to be burned. But somehow it doesn't seem as important as the fact that even something like this does not change people's basic attitudes."

MISS KEY SAID that at the time of the Watts rioting she observed that she had not run across any examples of that kind of thinking in Riverside, because the people who are trying to do something about the Negroes' problems are

Mrs. Banks said several parents of children who attend Lowell that she has talked to in the last two days have seemed satisfied with the school board's proposal to have children attend Lowell for about three weeks on double sessions until they can be transferred to other schools in the city.

Max Ullom, representing the education committee of the Human Relations Council, said he is contacting the executive committees of the various civil rights organizations in the area to meet at 8 p.m. tomorrow to discuss what can be done about the lack of communication among city officials, leaders of civil rights organizations and the people themselves.

County counsel may leave post

By BILL JENNINGS

A salary impasse that may lead to the departure of County Counsel Ray T. Sullivan Jr., after 12 years in office, developed yesterday among members of the County Board of Supervisors.

Paul Anderson and William Crook urged acceptance of a recommended salary increase schedule submitted by Personnel Director Donald E. Spencer and Administrative Officer Robert Andersen.

A board majority, Chairman William Jones, Norman Davis and Floyd McCall, supported a modified increase that fell below what Sullivan said he felt was the minimum the office is entitled to, and implied he may not stay if the last recommendation is not accepted.

HE LATER told reporters he had no comment on the situation other than to say: "Wait until Sept. 10."

RAY SULLIVAN
... Feels he's underpaid

parable counties, San Diego, Orange, San Bernardino, Fresno and Kern, indicated an October, 1964, average of $1,822, and an average today of $1,

Few leads in burning of school

By LEE SHORT

Investigation indicates the fire that burned Lowell School yesterday started inside the building on the floor under the window facing Cridge Street, says Battalion Chief Charles Brague, head of fire investigation.

But Brague said he could not tell at this time whether someone threw something through the window or gained entrance to the building to start the fire.

He said glass and a jar lid dug from debris under the window is being tested in the laboratory to determine what it had been used for. He said teachers at Lowell were being questioned to determine if the materials were used in the classrooms during the school year.

The chief fire marshall said he knew of no extra precautions being taken at Irving School or other buildings in the area of the Lowell fire and the fire department had not advised police on extra precautions.

"The police and the Division of Forestry are working very tightly with the Riverside fire department in the investigation and each is aware of the situation and what the other agencies are doing so there is no need for us to advise them, said Brague.

On whether the fire was set by children or adults, Brague said the fire department had not even conjectured on this. No tie in with several other recent arson cases is suspected, said Brague. He said this would only be looked into

Heated protests at meet

By TOM PATTERSON

The Riverside school board, on recommendation of Supt. Bruce Miller, voted yesterday to open burned-out Lowell School Monday with double sessions in classrooms not damaged by the fire.

The solution was proposed as strictly temporary while the administration looks for classrooms and teachers in other schools with a view toward transferring Lowell pupils to other schools.

The other schools, it was stipulated by Supt. Bruce

(Today a group of parents announced plans to boycott Lowell and Irving schools. See story, Page A-1)

Miller and Board President Arthur L. Littleworth, would not include nearby Irving School.

The action came amid heated charges and counter-charges about purposely-set boundaries to secure segregation at Lowell and Irving, about quality of education children are receiving at Lowell. Both whites and Negroes were in the audience and disputed board contentions.

THE BOARD acted after a two-hour meeting with a group of 30 or more residents of the Lowell-Irving area, who presented a petition asking that the two schools be closed. It had been circulated before the fire.

The board rejected the militant insistence that it act now for a permanent

READY TO GO—Developer Hunter Penn (right) yesterday won the right to make good his claim that he will give Riverside its first regional shopping center on a 66-acre site at Tyler and Magnolia. Eaton Ballard, vice president of the Broadway Department Store chain, told the Riverside City Council that his store was waiting only for the zoning to be granted before completing design work and beginning construction on the Tyler site. O. P. Ladd (left) is Penn's local representative and executive of M and G Properties.

WANTS TO TRY—Marcus W. Meairs (left) is still in the race to develop a regional shopping center for the Riverside area after receiving an

---

The Press, *Wednesday September 8, 1965, C (local) section, page 1. In addition to stories on the arson, the reporting on the crisis includes a boldfaced note in the School Board meeting article regarding plans for a boycott.*

---

more potential problems in that arrangement. The other alternative was to take the Lowell children and integrate them completely throughout the other schools in the system. Take the incoming Lowell kindergarten class and the first and second grade classes, about 250 children, and transport them to other schools. Thus the other schools would get four or five Lowell children in each of the kindergarten, first, and second grade classes. We decided on this plan. We thought that would be a start toward integration.

I had been on the phone throughout the day to the other Board members, and by Wednesday evening I had the general consent of the full Board to the plan for the displaced children. This plan would not address the petition to close both Lowell and Irving Schools. That would take more time and thought. But I had authority to say what the schools would do about the immediate problem. This authority would be vital when subsequent meetings took place Thursday and Friday.

Wednesday —
The Boycott

Beginning that Tuesday, I was hardly in my law office except just to pass through, for quite a long period of time. Wednesday, as we worked in the administration office to see what could be done to house the children displaced by the fire, we began to hear about the beginning of a boycott movement. It wasn't clear to us whether the boycott had been generated by the fact that we had not given the petitioners a satisfactory answer on the placement of children whose classrooms had been burned, or whether it was about the larger issue of the closing of the two schools. In either case, reports came in that a boycott was mounting and picking up momentum at tremendous speed.

As the week progressed, the situation was getting more serious. It was clear that we had to do something and do it quickly. The Watts riots in Los Angeles had started with police arrest of Marquette Frye, a 21-year-old black man, for drunk driving. His mother got involved and fought the arresting officer, tearing the officer's shirt. Another officer then struck Marquette's head with his nightstick. By the time the Fryes were arrested, hundreds of onlookers were drawn to the scene. Anger and rumors spread through the black community, and the next day the riots had begun. At the time, I was not familiar with the origins of the Watts riots and fires, but I did know that a forest fire might be the result of a tiny spark. It was critical to make sure the handling of plans for the Lowell children displaced by the fire did not ignite a large-scale conflict.

We began to get reports of threats and violence. For instance a Mexican-American woman said that there had been a note posted on her front door that said if her children went to school on Monday her house would be burned. The black janitors in all of the affected schools came to us and told us that they had been warned to stay out of the schools on Monday. There were other indications that a boycott was going to be enforced by threats to the community. Apparently Mayor Lewis was threatened. I don't know the full scope of what the police department knew, but the net result was that the mayor's house, my house, and Mr. Miller's house were under police surveillance for some period of time. My children, Anne and Todd, when they returned for the start of school, also had police protection. Anne attended Gage Junior High School and Todd was at Alcott School.

There were things we deliberately did not make public to the community. It seemed to me that if the community knew we were beginning to get threats of force and violence, from both the minority and majority populations, it was only going to make the situation more difficult to control.

I knew that violence was the kind of thing that would most likely attract television attention. As a matter of fact we did attract two television programs, and for each one I tried to play down the situation in Riverside so they would think that Riverside was not a newsworthy place to visit again. It had been my thought that the Watts situation had been made worse by the television coverage with the endless repetition of the most dramatic events. Some reporters saw the riots as the night's entertainment saying, "Everything is very quiet but just wait until tonight folks. Tune in tonight."

There was information that came to us, although I don't know how accurate it was, that the boycott would be accompanied by picket lines. The pickets would prevent children who wanted to go to school from going to their classes. This, it seemed to me, was a highly dangerous strategy. I later told Mr. Renfro that if that's what happened we would have no choice but to see that the children who wanted to go to school went through the picket lines, and that they would be escorted with whatever protection was necessary. It was ironic to be in the position of asserting that we would guarantee all children access to school even though it might be through potential picket lines of black protestors, when the norm during the civil rights era had been black school children being escorted through white crowds blocking their entry.

In place of public schools, the minority community had established "Freedom Schools" that would be held in churches and community buildings during the boycott. These included Amos Temple of CME Church, First Church of God, AME Church, Unitarian Church, All Saints Episcopal Church, and the Masonic Hall. The teachers were volunteers, including two college teachers and some college graduate students.

Thursday —
Meeting with the Boycott Leaders

When I finally got home that Wednesday night, I had a call from Ruth Bratten, whom I had known for some time. She was active in the League of Women voters, one of the organizers of the Human Relations Council, and was in good standing both with the minority communities and the community of Riverside at large. Ruth said that the situation was deteriorating very, very rapidly and that if something wasn't done we would have another Watts. She was convinced that the only person who could do anything to save the situation was me. She said, "The minority leaders will speak to you alone, but I don't think they will talk to anyone else." She suggested that I try to get in touch with Jesse Wall and see if I could work through him to establish a meeting with the minority leaders. On that Wednesday the situation was such that there really was no communication at all. The leaders of the minorities had said previously that they wouldn't talk to us. I tried to reach Jesse Wall. Ruth Bratten had given me his private, unlisted number, but I wasn't able to get him Wednesday night. I tried again Thursday morning. Again he was not in. I left a message at his house that I wanted to try to set up a meeting. Finally I received a call back from Mr. Bland. He said they would meet with me alone. I suggested that we have lunch together at a restaurant. He said no, he wanted me to come to the boycott headquarters. He explained where it was, and it turned out to be Mr. Renfro's house, in the garage. I agreed that I would meet them there at about 12:30 p.m. on Thursday.

I checked with the other Board members and then went to the Dunes restaurant for an early quick lunch. I was with several other lawyers from my firm, and they were concerned about my attending the meeting alone. Gene Nazarek, a former basketball player, 6'8" in height, wanted to come with me, and Bill De Wolfe, though smaller in stature, wanted to drive me. But I was concerned that we show no expression of fear. We needed to build trust.

While I was at lunch I was paged by the police department. When I answered the phone it was the chief of police, and he said he understood that I was going to go to a meeting at Mr. Renfro's house. How he found out, I don't know, but he asked me to stop by and see him before going to the meeting. When I got to the police department, the chief investigator of the Lowell fire was there, as well as Officer Etienne Caroline. The Chief told me that things were serious and he wanted to know if there was anything that I could promise them in the way of bringing about some relief. I told him that we had developed a plan for the children at Lowell. I thought it was as good a plan as possibly could be developed in a day's time. I had the authority to announce that, and I was going to do it. He said to go ahead, but he wanted Officer Caroline to attend the meeting. Officer Caroline was a black, plainclothes officer.

It took about 15 to 20 minutes for everyone to arrive, and we then went out on the patio of Mr. Renfro's house. There were about a dozen people in attendance. I knew Renfro, Bland, Alice Key, and Jess Ybarra from the Settlement House. I didn't know the rest of the people or whether they were local or from out of town. We settled into chairs on the patio. The air was still, the summer heat lingering and adding to the tension that was evident. I looked around trying to assess the feelings and direction this discussion might take. And as I looked, I spied a little boy sitting up in a tree, watching us all. It struck me as a humorous and somewhat bizarre counterpoint to the critical meeting ahead.

We had a long meeting. I think it lasted until three or four o'clock. And a great many things were discussed. I explained the plan that had been developed for the children who had been displaced by the fire. My sense was that this was satisfactory, but only because nobody complained about it. Nobody said it was okay either. So there wasn't much discussion about it.

There was, however, considerable discussion about the petition, and they were pressing for a lot of decisions on integration itself. I said, "You know we can't make

Ruth [Bratten] Anderson Wilson: *I was very active with the League of Women Voters, and was on John Sotelo's advisory committee. I ran for office in Ward 2 after he retired from the council. So I was very involved in the [Eastside] community. The councilman, John Sotelo, called me and said, "Ruth, something has got to be done. The town is in real bad shape. They're planning a boycott. They're meeting in secret. Things are smoldering. You're the only person in this whole town that both sides trust."*

[When I spoke with leaders in the black community] they said to me, "We need to talk to the school board chairman. Can you set up a meeting with our people and the school board chairman?"

I said, "Well I can ask him."

I talked to Art and he listened to me and said, "Is this very serious?"

I said, "This is very serious. Would you consider talking to these people because they are going to do a boycott of the schools? They need to be talked to about it. They don't want to do it, but they've got to do something. The people are looking to their leaders and saying to their leaders, 'Black leaders, you're not doing anything. We want to see some action.'"

They did that [initiated the Watts riots as a protest] over in LA. So that's why Sotelo called me . . . . When I talked to Art about this I said, "Would you consider talking to these people?"

[His response] was, "If you want to go ahead and set it up, I will do that." I told him I would get back to him.

He was in a heavy meeting. He left word, the only message that should come through on the telephone is from Mrs. Bratten. When I called him, he said, "What do you have?"

I said, "They want to see you."

"Fine," he said. He finished what he was doing. This was back and forth. They wanted to drive around in a car, an automobile, because they [didn't trust that] they would not be bugged.

"They want to travel in a car."

"Can you assure me of my safety?"

I said, "I know all three of these men, and they are all gentlemen." So that's what Art agreed to do.

They were trying to avoid a boycott of the schools. Art wanted them to stop the boycott. The boycott had already been announced. They had to go ahead, because if they didn't go through with the boycott they would lose face with their own people. It's understandable.

What they had said to me was, "They talk a lot, these white guys, but they don't do anything. They shelve it and then it gets bad again. If he really thinks he can do something, or intends to do something, then he must do it right away. It should not be stalled."

RUTH [BRATTEN] ANDERSON WILSON
COMMUNITY LEADER

Ruth [Bratten] Anderson Wilson moved to Riverside in 1954, and became an early member, then president, of the League of Women Voters. She chaired the committee that formed the Human Relations Commission, and held leadership positions in the YWCA and Urban League. She was involved in fair housing issues and served on many civic planning committees. In 1966, she was named, with Arthur Littleworth and Riverside City Manager John Wentz, as an Outstanding Citizen for 1966.

She is known for her environmental activism and with her friend Martha McLean, was instrumental in saving the Santa Ana River from being channelized. She was a founding member of the Tri-County Conservation League in 1966 and Clean Air Now, in the 1970s. She has served on the board of the Rubidoux Community Services District since 1998.

. . . Wilson continued on page 51

those decisions at this time." By this time I had become well aware of the problems that had happened previously, and that sometimes people had made promises under stress that they couldn't keep. So I kept saying, "No, we can't do this," and "We can't do that." Those were not happy responses and they didn't sit well with the group. Finally we got around to the boycott.

I reminded them that we had what appeared to be a good solution to the fire, and that the Board would move as fast as circumstances permitted on the petition itself. I was hopeful that they would call off the boycott. They said no, they were not about to call off the boycott.

I can't remember how this came about, but there was an indication that there could be violence if we didn't just give them what they wanted. This was a crucial moment. I remember at that time thinking, "I'm not sure that this is the right thing to say but I think I have to speak plainly." I said, "I don't want you to underestimate me. We've been trying for a couple of years and we thought we were doing the right thing with your support. Now you're telling us that it wasn't the right thing to do, and that something has got to be changed. Well, we're willing to listen and talk, and we want to do what is right. But," I said, "don't threaten us. If you think you are going to get this by threats, you've got another think coming. We will meet force with force."

I waited to see what was going to happen. Nothing did.

But they still weren't ready to call off the boycott. At least there were some people who seemed to have no real desire to call it off no matter what happened. They wanted a fight. The others said they could not call off the boycott because they were not the leaders; they were what were called "coordinators." I argued with them that if they had started the boycott it seemed to me that they could stop it, but they said they could not. They said that if anyone was going to be able to stop it, it would have to be me. People would not believe them, if they repeated what I said. If anything was to be accomplished I would have to say it directly to their people, and they wanted to know if I would come to such a meeting.

I didn't tell them at that point that I would attend, as I had some doubts about it. First because the meeting was going to be under their control, and it obviously was going to be a very large meeting. They wanted to invite the whole Eastside community. I was concerned about what might happen at a very large meeting if it broke up with anger, as had happened at the Tuesday Board meeting. Secondly, I didn't know how it was going to be run, or who was going to be running it. I came back, talked with the chief of police and with Bruce Miller, Ray Berry, City Manager John Wentz, and Mayor Ben Lewis. Nobody particularly liked the idea of the meeting, but it seemed necessary if we had any chance of calling off the boycott—and perhaps the violence that would go with it. We concluded that we should go ahead and attend.

Wilson continued from page 49

I said this emphatically to Art, more than one time, I'm afraid. "Art whatever you do, make sure it begins to happen right away." He did that. He was severely criticized for it. But it showed [the boycott leaders] they could trust his word, he was willing to work with them.

He felt, the same way we all did, that the integration of schools was severely behind in the city.

He was criticized and he stood his ground the whole time. My part was to get it started. One white man, three black men. Talking to each other. Listening to each other. Agreeing to make the integration of the system start now. He promised to do it. He said he would start it right away. And he did. He never, never went back on it.

I remember George Williams, he was one of them, saying they talked man to man. It didn't matter who was black and who was white, who was tall and who was short, they talked man to man. My part was over when the men met.

Date	*Sept 18*	Time	*8.30*
To	*all*		

WHILE YOU WERE OUT

M *Ruth Bratton*

of _____

Phone *686 9940*

TELEPHONED	✓	PLEASE CALL	✓
CALLED TO SEE YOU		WILL CALL AGAIN	
WANTS TO SEE YOU		RETURNED CALL	

MESSAGE *Urgent*

Jess Wall
OV 32028

Above: Phone message from Ruth Bratten, setting up the meeting with the boycott leaders.

Friday Morning —
Meeting with the Teachers

For a long time, we had planned a general meeting of all of our teachers and principals on the upcoming Friday. It was scheduled for the Ramona High School auditorium and it was full. Well over 1,000 teachers and administrators were there. It was supposed to be a rally to start the school year with enthusiasm, and this was the first time we had ever had a meeting of this kind. Both Mr. Miller and I were scheduled to speak. I recall my assignment was to discuss the curriculum for the coming year and how federal financing fitted in, but it became apparent that this was very inappropriate on this particular morning.

So I tore up my notes and spoke without preparation. I simply told them in detail what had happened during the Labor Day weekend and on Tuesday, Wednesday, and Thursday, leaving out the part that dealt with the threats of violence and force. I told them that the situation was serious and what the Board proposed to do about it. The plan to take care of the Lowell children displaced by the fire would be made public at a meeting at Irving School that night. I was hopeful that at that meeting we would be able to convince the minority leaders of our sincerity, to get them to accept the plan, and to gain sufficient time to decide what to do about the basic petition itself. But the boycott was still on, and I told the teachers they would have to be prepared for whatever was going to happen.

Barbara Shackelton, now a very good friend, was a young teacher who had been recruited from Wisconsin, and she was at the meeting. She remembers well the information I was giving had a calming effect on her and those around her.

This Ramona meeting was most fortuitous and beneficial. It was the beginning of the process of gaining the faculty's support.

Friday Noon —
Urgency: Promise Only What We Can Do

Friday at a luncheon meeting, the full Board met with Bruce Miller and Ray Berry. We made preparations for the mass meeting at Irving School that night. Mr. Berry, the associate superintendent, would go with me. Mr. Miller, the superintendent of schools and head of administration, was too closely identified in the minds of the minority community with the past failures of the school system and therefore would not attend. This criticism of Mr. Miller was mostly unjustified, but the fact of the matter was that Mr. Berry was the only administrator the minority community trusted.

I reviewed at length Thursday's meeting at Mr. Renfro's home, including the use of force to protect the children who wished to attend school, if necessary. The plan for

ROBERT BLAND
COMMUNITY LEADER, LOWELL PARENT

Robert Bland was born and raised in Virginia where the schools he attended were totally segregated. He applied to the University of Virginia, even though he knew it was a white and predominantly male school, because it was the premier academic institution in the state. Though a very few black men and women had been accepted to graduate school in law, medicine, and education, Robert Bland was in the first undergraduate class of three African Americans, entering the engineering program in 1955.

Bland chose electrical engineering as his major. While accepted without differential treatment in the classroom, the three African Americans were isolated in terms of the university's social life and Bland's two black classmates left in spring of 1956.

Bland's experience at the university demonstrated to him that minority schools in Virginia were not teaching at the same level as white schools and there was significant coursework in math and science missing from his high school education. He persevered and became the first African-American graduate in engineering in 1959. After graduation, he went to work for the Naval Ordnance Laboratory in Corona. Later, he moved to Newbury Park and worked for the Naval Weapons System Engineering Station at Port Hueneme where he was department manager of Missile and Launching Systems. The year before Lowell burned, his daughter, Angela, had been in Esther [Velez] Andrews kindergarten class.

Robert Bland: *What happened was that there were a number of us who had worked in John Sotelo's campaign to become the first minority councilman in Riverside, so we had a nucleus of people who were interested in what was going on in Riverside from the standpoint of civil rights. I remember a meeting at Irving School with an administrator; he was leading the discussion about how minority students were doing in what was a de facto segregated school system. And being an administrator, he had access to test scores. He was able to show us exactly what was happening with these students in terms of their performance on standardized tests. And the thing he was pointing out was that there was obviously a gap in performance between minority students and the white students.*

The interesting thing he pointed out was that the gap started out very small and each school year the gap grew bigger and bigger. So that when these students left elementary school, they found themselves academically far behind the students they were competing with in the middle school environment.

We were obviously troubled by what we were seeing and that was the first time that we approached the school board about this problem. We realized, of course, that we were operating within the environment of a de facto segregated school system but that was not of primary importance to us at that time, what was really important were the achievement levels. So we said, "What can we do about these achievement levels? What is it that we can do to help close these gaps so that these students will be able to be successful in their school experience?"

That was when we [parents, board, and administrators] helped to come up with a plan for Compensatory Education. That was our first attack at the problem. Jess Wall was involved at the time, Art was obviously involved, and Ray Berry. As I recall, Ray Berry was the assistant superintendent. The superintendent was Bruce Miller. He was not very helpful. As a matter of fact he found himself in opposition to most of what we wanted to do. Ray, on the other hand, was helpful, understanding, and cooperative. He and Art were the primary forces that were working with us, instead of against us, in this whole effort.

So we launched off on this path of Compensatory Education, and it didn't really work out all that great. . . .It was a combination of a lot of things, but the end result was that we weren't making any headway. The problem we were trying to solve proved too intransigent to overcome through the measures that were being taken. So folks like us, who were kind of on the outside looking in, we didn't see changes happening in terms of standardized test scores. [We also didn't see] the kinds of things we thought needed to happen to make that change, or at least happening to the degree that we thought would make the difference.

That led to a lot of dissatisfaction among people in the community who had been involved in this process from the beginning. Also, one of the other undercurrents was that there was a faction in the community who kind of thought we had sold out in the beginning by not asking for desegregation of the schools but [instead] going along with a program of Compensatory

. . . Bland continued on page 55

Irving School Auditorium

the children displaced by the fire was authorized. The petition was going to come up again at the Board's Monday meeting, and we had no answer. We could not delay the fate of Lowell and Irving Schools very long, but I suggested a 30-day cooling off period during which time we would develop a workable plan.

By Friday I had become convinced of several things. One was that if we were going to do anything at all that would be constructive, we had to do it promptly. Secondly, I had come to realize that there was a tremendous lack of understanding and a lack of trust between the minority people and not only the school system but also any level of government.

This complete lack of trust stunned me. I had no idea any appreciable percentage of our population felt that way. They had accused the School District in some of the earlier meetings of breaking faith with a number of things and promising things that hadn't been carried out. For the most part I think this was not true. Nevertheless I began to realize the importance of not promising more in the pressure of the moment than we would ultimately be able to deliver. It was important that we promise only that which we were absolutely sure we could do. And then we had to keep our promises.

I knew that we were not in a position to be able to take legal action until the School Board meeting on Monday, but I also knew that at this point the minority community didn't understand that. The meeting at Irving School was their meeting. They wanted answers, they wanted quick answers, and they looked to the president of the School Board as the person who ought to be able to give those answers. If I didn't give an answer, they would feel the schools were avoiding the complaint.

Bland continued from page 53

Education. So, certainly an element in the community had been dissatisfied from the start at the approach that we were taking. That, of course, only intensified as the Compensatory Education Program continued to produce no tangible results in terms of the measures that we were looking at.

We finally made the decision that we were going to approach the school board about forgetting about the Compensatory Education and going for the integration of the schools by whatever means were necessary. That's when we started the petition drive. Those of us who were involved, we went door to door. . . and got signatures of parents and community members asking the school board to fully integrate the schools.

We were scheduled to go in and present the petitions to the school board [on the Tuesday after Labor Day]. The school burning was a dramatic enough event anyway, but it occurred within the context and the same time frame of the Watts Riots in LA. And so, it added some drama to the whole thing. I don't know if it was helpful or hurtful in terms of the impact that it had, but it certainly heightened the drama surrounding it.

So we went in with the petitions, and there wasn't any real action taken by the school board at that time. . . . The actions that went on that day were not conclusive in any way. You left there feeling, "Yes, they let us get up and speak but nothing's going to really come of this." The urgent problem, of course, was what to do with the students who had formerly attended Lowell but the bigger problem was what was going to be done with regard to integration of the schools. We didn't feel that we got any indication that there was going to be serious consideration of our request to integrate the schools. That was the impression we came away from that meeting with, and that certainly colored the discussions we had in our meetings following that school board meeting.

That was why we felt it was necessary to organize a boycott of the schools and that was the task we set ourselves to in those next few days, going around again, door to door, to people in the community asking them not to send their kids to school the first day of school and also trying to set up what we called Freedom Schools. Those would be a short-term alternative for as long as the boycott needed to last.

I know that [Bruce Miller] was not in favor of it [integration] at all, and he was not reticent to say so whenever he got the opportunity, either in public or in private. I am sure that influenced our perception of what was going to happen as well.

By the time of [the Thursday, September 9th meeting with Art Littleworth], the impetus for the whole boycott was in motion, and to stop that, certainly on our part, would have required something tangible, to go back to the community and say, "Let's call this off" . . . but without anything concrete to be able to offer [we weren't going to take the pressure off].

We talked a lot during that whole timeframe with Art and with Ray and with other members of the school board, usually in small groups, from the time we began the process with Compensatory Education and all the way through. That was the good thing in the whole process, that we did talk. I was happy about the idea that we were talking and I certainly felt that Art, personally, wanted to do the right thing. . . . I think we all thought that [we were trying to do the right thing with the Compensatory Education Program] in the beginning, but it didn't work. . . . I have a general impression that we kind of caught them by surprise . . . that they were saying to us, "We thought we sat down and agreed to this program and here you are back telling us that's not what you want. Why did you change your mind?"

I think we felt all the way along that they understood the problem; I don't think they shared the same view that we did about what the solution was. At this point our solution was integration of the schools, and we had made up our minds that we were not going to be deterred from that objective. It might not happen, but that was always going to be what we asked for, what we were going to seek, and we were going to try to put as much pressure on the school board to do that as we could, by any means that we could, through petitions, boycott, Freedom Schools, and whatever else.

My recollection of the Irving School meeting [September 10th] is [that] a lot of different things were coming to the fore at that point. We had a core of people whose primary concern was, "How do we solve the educational issue of closing that gap between the achievement of minority kids and the general population?" Now that we were getting down to specifics, a whole new set of issues were coming up, "What's going to happen to my child in this whole mess? If they are going to be moved to a different school, what's going to happen to them, how are they going to be treated? How am I going to get them there? What happens if they get sick and they need to come home?"

. . . Bland continued on page 57

Friday Evening — Meeting at Irving School

At eight o'clock on Friday evening I went to Irving School accompanied by Ray Berry. It was an overflow meeting with people standing around the sides and in the back of the auditorium. The mayor was in attendance although he did not speak. Board members Sharp and Stern also sat in the audience. Tom Patterson of *The Press-Enterprise* was there, and he would write an article on the meeting without alluding to the emotional and volatile tone of the speakers. I don't know how many people the auditorium seated, but there were easily several hundred.

This was the first time that we saw any evidence that non-Riversiders were involved in the boycott movement or in Riverside's racial problems. There were a number of people I had never seen before, and some of them later identified themselves as being from out of town. From what the police told me later, they were members of various civil rights organizations from other parts of the state, and indeed, from outside of California.

One of the organizations represented was CORE, the Congress of Racial Equality. These non-Riversiders came to speak, and they became a large part of the meeting. CORE was founded in Chicago in 1942 originally as a pacifist group. It spread nationally with active chapters in most major urban centers. In the South it focused on non-violent civil disobedience to challenge racial segregation laws. Outside of the South, CORE's emphasis was on discrimination in employment and housing and in *de facto* school segregation. But by the mid-1960s black nationalist sentiments were emerging within CORE, and in 1966, those ideas would lead to the formation of the Black Panther Party. The Black Panther Party chose separation, not integration, of schools.

The presence of outsiders was most disappointing because I felt that there was no way to reach these people. They had not seen our commitment in 1963 to upgrade the education of minorities, or the Compensatory Education Program, or indeed, the 1963 minority community's rejection of integration in Riverside in favor of neighborhood schools.

As the meeting progressed, people pointed their fingers at me and said, "Don't you trust that man one bit. Don't you believe anything he says! These are promises we have heard before, and nothing will happen!" It became clear we would be held responsible for some of the injustices which had occurred in places throughout the whole country. There was simply no trust in our system.

In any event, the meeting began with my being introduced by the chairwoman, Mrs. Josephine Stewart. I explained the plan which the Board had authorized me to put forth, which was basically the taking care of the children displaced by the fire. The plan was to take about 250 Lowell School children in the kindergarten, first, and second

Bland continued from page 55

It was a turbulent time. There were a lot of things going on. It wasn't that long after the school burning, the confrontation with the school board, the concern—particularly of Lowell parents—about what was going to happen to their kids, were they going to be well taken care of and treated appropriately? It was a time of frustration and general emotion, and it was unfocused and didn't have a lot of direction. People were saying a lot of conflicting things. I can understand Art's feelings about it. I was having some of the same feelings myself.

I was very much involved [in organizing the Freedom Schools]. There was a doctor in town, Percy Baugh, and we kind of put Percy in charge of being principal of the Freedom Schools. I was involved in going out and finding places we could meet, a lot of churches, the Masonic Hall. It was kind of eye opening to me how many churches turned us down, didn't want to take a position in this controversy, and which churches welcomed us. I helped to find the places, helped to recruit the teachers, and helped to get the word out to people about what was going to happen and where they should take their kids.

[The boycott] was only one day, because there was a school board meeting that night [Monday, September 13th]. I remember the superintendent getting up and saying that 90 percent of the students were in school—his attempt to minimize the effects of the boycott and say that the boycott was not having an effect on the schools. That was a pivotal meeting, because it was the basis on which we made the decision in the community to end the boycott.

I was not in favor of ending the boycott at that point. I was skeptical. We heard the school board say, "We have a commitment to [integration]," but as far as concrete steps that had been taken, I didn't feel that there were any. My position was that we ought to wait until we see something more concrete before we end this boycott, but I was in the minority that evening. The bulk of the people were in favor of ending what was a difficult operation, the Freedom Schools. They were ready to bring that to an end, so we made that decision, called off the boycott and closed the Freedom Schools.

I was okay with it but I had my fingers crossed and was holding my breath that what had seemed like a commitment was actually carried through by the board. I don't think that I doubted the sincerity on the part of Art and Ray Berry, who were people that I perceived had been most helpful along this whole process, but whether they could move the whole school administration . . . was where my skepticism came from.

Rather than being less skeptical, I think for other people in the community it was, "This is too hard. Let's not continue to do this, let's see what happens. We may have to do something again later, but for now, let's go along and see." There were some people who were confident, like Jess Wall, because he was part of the system. And there were other people who had some confidence. But I think among the leadership, I don't think many of us were confident, but we were willing to give it a try.

There was resistance in the beginning. I remember after the decision was made, that there were a lot of parents' groups in previously all-white neighborhoods that met to address their concerns about what was going on. I know that Art had to go and speak to a number of these groups. I remember being at a meeting where there was a group of parents kind of grilling him about why [the school board members] were making the decision they were. There were a couple of us, at the back of the room. The [white parents] were saying, "Why is it that these parents want these kids to go to our schools?" And Art said, "They're standing right back there, why don't you ask them?" And so we came up and spoke to them about what our concerns were and why we felt [integration] was the thing to do. It kind of tamped down any emotions, but I know that there were a number of those kinds of meetings going on around town.

There was a lot of emotion on both sides. [The Blands received both hate mail and threatening phone calls during this period.] . . . Part of the context was that this was all going on at the height of the civil rights movement. There was a general movement throughout the whole country of addressing inequities, particularly those based on race.

I think what happened in Riverside was unique. It was a unique combination of the times and the people involved that [made] what happened possible. If it hadn't been for the leadership of people like Art and Ray Berry on the school board side, and if it hadn't been for some of those new black urban professionals who had recently come to Riverside, if it hadn't been for the times we were going through and the heightened sensitivity that was created . . . what we had was a confluence of all of those things. Any one of those things by itself would have been unsuccessful but all of those things coming together at one time, in one place was why Riverside was able to become the first major school district to integrate the schools.

grades (and moving into the third grade if we could do so), and integrate those children completely throughout the other schools in the system where we had available space; to provide transportation; and to put the program into effect by mid-week of the first week of school. There were questions about this, but I think basically this phase of the program was well accepted.

I also asked for thirty days in which to consider the broader problems, that is, what should happen to Lowell and Irving Schools, and to make a report. I also said that no matter what would ultimately happen to the fourth, fifth and sixth graders, Lowell would not be rebuilt at that location.

Most of the questions, however, seemed to get more and more hostile as the meeting progressed. These were related to the problems of integration generally and to the problems of Lowell and Irving Schools in particular. In my responses I suggested that the School District's consideration of minority problems as a whole needed to take into account Casa Blanca, and that there were many other factors we needed to know.

Jesse Wall's leadership of the Compensatory Education Program had been questioned earlier, but this was the first time we had had serious complaints about the program itself. We needed to have time to find out for ourselves whether it was effective or it wasn't. We didn't know how representative the people attending this meeting were of the entire black community. And we knew virtually nothing about the desires and feelings of the Mexican-American community.

These were things that I felt we had to know before we could come up with an intelligent policy, and this was again part of the reason that I was asking for the thirty days. I can't remember whether October 18th turned out to be precisely thirty days, but I gave the date of October 18th as the date we would have a report.

Up until this time the meeting had been pretty much a question and answer session with me. But the format and tone of the meeting began to change with a lengthy and impassioned address by Joe Aguilar.[15] He basically said that the cause of the African American was the same as the cause of the Mexican American, and that his people should want precisely the same things. A tremendous ovation greeted Joe Aguilar's speech, and I think that in a sense his talk reached an emotional pitch that began to turn the meeting.

We began to have a series of volatile speeches but no more questions. I don't remember the order, but Dr. Percy Baugh, a black physician, gave a lengthy, emotional speech. He started out his remarks by saying, "Now I don't want you to think my remarks are incendiary but . . . " He went on to use an analogy that he had a granny who had told him that he would never get anything without a fight.

One speaker after another clearly was trying to whip up the group to fight. There was only one speaker who turned against this tide, and he got hooted down. He was Etienne Caroline, a black man, who the crowd knew was a detective on the police

---

15.   Mr. Aguilar was later elected to the Board of Trustees of the Riverside City College District.

JESSE WALL

TEACHER AND ADMINISTRATOR

Born in Mississippi, Jesse Wall moved to Texas and later, at 9 years of age, to Riverside where he attended Longfellow School, University Heights Junior High School, and Riverside Polytechnic High School. He started college at Riverside City College and went on to California State University, Los Angeles, graduating as a teacher. In 1959, he became the first black high school teacher in Riverside, teaching at the new Ramona High School. That year, he was also elected president of the Riverside NAACP.

In 1964, he began to work full-time in the district's administrative offices, directing the Compensatory Education Program with Richard Purviance, principal at Lowell School. After Lowell was burned, Jesse Wall became director of Intergroup Education, supporting the implementation of integration. In that capacity, he worked with Esther [Velez] Andrews, Bea Pavitt, and Ernest Robles.

He was also assistant to his father, pastor of St. James Church of God in Christ. The church purchased the Lowell School site after the fire and converted the kindergarten building to house the church. In the late 1980s, the balance of the site was developed by the church as affordable senior housing, J. E. Wall Victoria Manor.

Jesse Wall: *Some of the basis of hostility had to do with a decision the school district made. [I] don't know where the pressure came from to make that decision but what happened is that we built a new school, Alcott. Lowell was a balanced attendance area because many . . . kids on Prince Albert Drive were students there. Then all of a sudden students from those streets went to Alcott, and Lowell School became primarily black and Hispanic. What was bothersome to a lot of people is that they had made sure they were living [in the Lowell attendance area] so their kids would attend an integrated school.*

The biggest meeting was at Irving School. We had professional blacks—doctors and engineers. We had the CORE people. We had some clergy.

Josie was chairing the meeting. Arthur Littleworth, and Ray Berry, and I, representing the school district, are under the gun. Ray Berry, he turns to me and he says, "Jess, I hate to tell you, but tonight you are going to be the scapegoat, because we are going to offer you as the item that we have done, or put into action: naming you as director of Compensatory Education. That places you on the spot."

When [people at the Irving School meeting] said, "You didn't do this, you didn't do that [referring to the school district's efforts]," he pointed to me and said, "This is the man who has been given the authority to get things together."

They said, "We know what he did, but what he did was not enough." And so, that meeting was the turning point in our district's effort to provide quality education to all of the children in Riverside.

Arthur Littleworth was gifted with temperance. He was soft spoken. . . . He would get to the heart of the matter and deal with it factually, without emotions. He never would utter a statement like "You people." Even though from the audience, from [the community] side of the table, we were saying, "You people." He would never retort.

Art and Ray were conciliatory. They listened to pick up the tone. They were proactive. They did not defend themselves except to say that we are aware of the problem because of Mr. Wall over here, and we are continuing to work, and happy to find out about your true feelings.

My job was to talk to the parents to sensitize them to their responsibility and also facilitate for them. What [the school board] did was provide us with a budget so we could create a department that dealt with the integration program.

We had some stormy days. We had fistfights between parents and teachers. My office was like the firemen's office. [I would get the call] to go put the fire out. I would let Ray Berry know. Ernest Robles was attending to the Hispanic communities. We had threats. Kids coming home and complaining.

We had [about a dozen] school-community workers. I was looking for people who could either start a riot or stop a riot. They had to be outspoken

. . . Wall continued on page 61

force. My responses to the questions in the meeting had included a review of earlier actions by the School Board. And Caroline indicated that what I had said about what had happened in the last couple of years had been true. He asked the group to consider giving us the thirty days. He was shouted down.

There was another speaker who said that he was paid to take care of matters of this kind. He had recently come from the East and had been through lots of things like this, and he was there to tell the crowd that there was a national conspiracy against the black man. He said the white man was afraid to let the African American get out from underneath his control; that if the blacks ever competed on even terms with the white man that would be the end of the white man. He went on to say that there was only one thing to do and that was to fight. That Riverside was now ready to fight and they should not miss the opportunity.

In the crowded room, people were jostled and elbowed as the speakers tried to get to the microphone. The meeting lost any semblance of order and the tension was rising. One speaker after another tried to stir up the crowd to enforce the boycott. People grabbed the microphone and harangued the audience urging them to action with shouts of support in the background. Even with a microphone it became difficult to hear as the crowd was getting louder and louder. Each speaker seemed to incite the next and the situation was escalating.

This was becoming an explosive situation. The chairwoman, Mrs. Josephine Stewart, had clearly lost control. She urged me to leave, and I was having similar thoughts. Rational discussion was no longer possible, and I feared violence. But leaving the meeting would be tricky. I didn't want my leaving to be a cause for disrespect. So I announced that I was leaving so that a decision could be made without our interference. Ray Berry and I left without any incident. The mayor also left at that point. We learned afterwards that they had taken a vote, and the vote had been on whether the boycott should be called off and if we should be given the thirty days. The vote was overwhelmingly in favor of continuing the boycott.

Friday Midnight —
Superintendent Miller's House

As I left the meeting at Irving School I was convinced that we were headed for violence. Actually, I didn't waste any time getting off the school grounds. It was the first time I felt frightened, and I was frightened not only for myself but for the community. The meeting was full of strangers. I did not know how many were out-of-towners, but they were strangers to the fact that the traditional minority leaders and the schools had been doing what they thought was right for the minority community—and that they could be trusted to deal with the petition quickly and with

Wall continued from page 59

individuals. We had male, female, Anglo, Hispanic and black on our staff. Each person hired had to have his or her own automobile. With students dispersed all over the city, if the parents had a parent conference, they had to have assistance getting there. We would go and pick them up and talk to them on the way about the problems, if there were any. Josie Samuels and Doris McCartney, they were two aides, great people in the community who helped us.

But overall, we had a very smooth transition. We never had protests or riots during the process of desegregating the schools. However, leading up to our decision to desegregate using busing, we had some stormy meetings we had to face.

After two or three years, it all leveled off and everyone was proud of Riverside. Being the first school district to do this, the district gave me permission to work with the state education department, Dr. Wilson Riles, and I was up in Sacramento about four or five times a month assisting the State Department of Education. I was invited to all kinds of meetings, all over the country, to talk about the Riverside story and what we were able to achieve with desegregation.

Above: Josephine Stewart chaired the community meeting, Friday, September 10, 1965 at Irving School. She later became a community aide in the Home-School Program that supported integration. During this period of time, she remarried and her name became Josephine Samuels.

understanding. I was concerned that the irrationality of the Watts riot and fires had displaced the admonition of Martin Luther King, Jr., that "We must not allow our creative protest to degenerate into physical violence."

I went to Bruce Miller's house and was joined by Ray Berry and Don Taylor. We discussed the situation at length, and somewhere around midnight I put through a call to City Manager John Wentz. I told him that I thought we were headed for possible violence with the opening of school and that we would have to take precautions. It looked as though the crisis had passed beyond anything the schools could deal with alone and that we had to treat it as a city problem. The result of my call was that we set up a meeting for Saturday at 8 a.m.

Saturday —
Meeting of All City and School Officials

The meeting at eight o'clock on Saturday morning was attended by all the city and school officials. Attending from the city were City Manager John Wentz; the city attorney, L.T. Kincaid; the chief of police; and Public Works Director Jim Martinek. From the schools, there was our own county counsel, Bruce Miller, Ray Berry, and the full Board of Education. We reviewed with the city people what had happened. They also had received a report from the police department about what had happened at the Irving School meeting. The chief of police said that from what he knew—and he apparently knew more than what had transpired at the Irving meeting—things were very serious. So we began to lay plans for what should be done on Monday, the first day of the new school year.

We first had to make a formal request to the City of Riverside for their assistance in taking over. The chief of police was directed to obtain back-up protection, first from the Riverside County Sheriff's Department, second from March Air Force Base, and third a preliminary contact with the National Guard.

We agreed that plainclothes policemen would be placed in all of the schools where we felt there might be problems. To the best of our ability we would not show any signs of force. We felt that if there were large squads of police around, and any other show of force, it would be more apt to incite violence than it was to prevent it. With the exception of the plainclothesmen, who were stationed with each principal, we had no police directly on the spot. School principals were later called in that day and given instructions—basically about how not to provoke an incident.

This city-school meeting went on for nearly three hours. The net result was that plans were developed both within the schools and within the city to take care of what appeared to be a strong likelihood that there would be violence at the opening of school.

Saturday Noon —
Meeting with *The Press-Enterprise* Newspaper

The Saturday meeting of city-school officials was held at the old school district administration building located at 12th and Locust Streets. (The Riverside Unified School District headquarters is now located at 14th and Lime Streets.) After the meeting, I made a spur-of-the-moment decision. I would walk over to *The Press-Enterprise* offices and tell them what was going on. *The Press-Enterprise* company published three editions of the newspaper at that time, all with slightly different names, *The Daily Enterprise* in the morning, *The Press* in the evening, and a single Sunday edition called the *Sunday Press-Enterprise.*

This is one of the best decisions I made throughout this crisis. I wanted to see Howard H. Hays, Jr., (Tim Hays), the editor. He was a graduate of Harvard Law School, though he had never practiced law. And he was a good friend. He was not in, but the assistant editor was. I didn't know Norm Cherniss very well then. Mr. Cherniss, unlike Tim Hays, was not active in community affairs, but I thought I could trust him. The paper had always done what was best for Riverside.

There was no agreement that our conversation was "off the record," but I reviewed in detail what had happened during the last few days. I said it probably was best for the community not to know about this, but I explained the threats of violence and the precautions both the city and school district were prepared to take. The situation was critical. Mr. Cherniss inquired about my own safety and that of my family. My wife and two children, Anne aged 13, and Todd aged 10, were still at the beach on an extended Labor Day—and I intended to keep them there. For myself, I intended to move out of our house since my bedroom was in the front of the house, a short distance from the street and an easy throw for a firebomb. I moved that Saturday night into the home of Charles D. Field, one of our young lawyers in the firm.

There was a reporter for the local newspapers who at that time covered all of the meetings of the School Board. He had been on that beat for years and I knew him well. Tom Patterson was his name. His reporting over the years gave me confidence in *The Press-Enterprise*, and he continued to cover the story of the crisis. It was reported to me, and I don't know whether it was true or not, that Howard H. Hays, Sr., the father of Tim, and the owner and president of *The Press-Enterprise*, had personally attended one of the protest meetings.

Throughout this situation, the local newspaper coverage was full, but responsible. There was no attempt to sensationalize the stories. And there was no coverage about the threats of violence, nor of what we were prepared to do about it.

Television Coverage

The first experience we had with television coverage was on the Thursday before school started. It was a Los Angeles station but not one of the big three: ABC, CBS or NBC. I had just returned from the Thursday meeting at Mr. Renfro's home, and as I walked into my office at Best Best & Krieger, there was a TV crew. Without an introduction, this fellow put a microphone in front of me and said, "Have you got a statement?" I said, "What in the world are you talking about?" After some conversation he said that he wanted a statement, " . . . just on the boycott situation." I remarked that I had just talked with a group of the leaders and we were working on a solution to the boycott. The television interviewer did not tell me at that time that he had been at Lowell School and had talked to a number of people who had specific complaints about the schools. When the first TV program came on the air, it showed several persons whom they had interviewed around Lowell School. Then they said, "And now we'll hear from the Board President," as if in response to those complaints. Of course, I had been given an entirely different subject, and my statement made no sense regarding their complaints. It was as if the Board President didn't care at all about the problems. An irresponsible TV station had just reinforced what the minorities had said about a governmental response.

My second experience with television was considerably better than the first. At noon on the first day of school, NBC-TV was present. They were at the "Freedom School," and they had interviewed a number of people. I was wary about being set up a second time. I asked who they had talked to and what these other people had said. I recited the TV experience of Thursday and they said that NBC didn't operate that way. They were very fair. We had about a ten- or fifteen-minute briefing session so I knew who they had spoken with, what they had found out, and therefore I could fashion my statement accordingly. I didn't see the coverage but I understand they showed actually about five minutes of it, and it was fair and responsible. But again our approach basically was to try to play down the problems. We tried to convince the TV people that Riverside didn't have so much news that they should bring a camera crew out every day.

Over the Weekend —
More Meetings, but No Resolution

There were many meetings and telephone calls over the weekend. Saturday afternoon Mr. Miller called in all of the school principals and some of the other people in the school system who would be involved. There were several other meetings on Saturday and on Sunday during which he was trying to alert the school people to the whole situation, and to coordinate school system efforts. Ray Berry met with African-American teachers at their request.

TYREE ELLISON
COMMUNITY MEMBER

Tyree Ellison's family came to Riverside in 1918.

He grew up on the Eastside and attended Irving School, University Heights Junior High School, and Riverside Polytechnic High School. He continued his education at Riverside City College.

He has been widely involved in community activities and had a decades-long career with Riverside County Probation Department. He worked with juvenile offenders at Juvenile Hall and was promoted to supervisor early in his career. He became the training officer, served for 13 years, and was responsible for training throughout the organization, including supervising the state audit process for training. Under his leadership, the training program became a model for other probation departments.

He served as president of the Eastside Community Action group and was involved in the development of Head Start programs locally. He believes strongly in community commitment and helping to make his community better for everyone.

Tyree Ellison: *It was terrible when I was a kid. The different theaters: the Fox Theater, the De Anza, the Del Rio, the Golden State . . . they put us in certain sections, up in the balcony. Segregation. . . . You know the area by Wheelock Field? My godfather, Mr. Streeter, had a picture of a Klan rally, there on the football field. I saw those pictures myself. . . . Right here, the [Eastside] area south of 14th, there were housing covenants. . . . My brothers had to leave Riverside to get a decent job.*

[During the early 60s] the old guard in the school system still controlled everything. Edna Lockhart, she worked at the school district for many years. She had a lot of power. Children were assigned to specific schools, and couldn't really transfer. . . . A lot of the mandates [like open enrollment] were slow being implemented.

When I heard the fire engines, I got up and went down. The school was on fire. That was when everyone started getting together. Because the school district had no plan. Where are we going to send the children to school? Retired teachers, everyone who had taught, teachers who were teaching in other places, everyone came together and supported putting temporary schools together.

At the time [Irving School meeting, September 10th], the parents didn't know where their kids were going to be placed, so there was a lot of frustration. They didn't know . . . whether [the district] would split them up. And that did happen, two kids, each going to a different school. That made it difficult, if the mother didn't have transportation because the bus service wasn't very viable at that time. They were upset.

There were other people that came here, that we didn't know. Evidently they had heard, I don't know how . . . through the grapevine out of L.A. or wherever. They had come to Riverside, and they were around and trying to find out what we were feeling. There were about three or four. We didn't know them that well, they were silent. You just knew that they weren't from around here. They never tried to become part of us anyway.

It kind of quieted down by the time of the Grant meeting [September 13th]. That was more of a sensible meeting. At that time we had some legal advice and it was more organized. There was a lot of give and take . . . It was the belief factor. Some people wanted to have things like they were before. [Some people wanted to keep the boycott going.] Eventually everyone came to the idea, "It's going to be okay, let's see how it works out." . . . It's the unknown that creates fear.

The timing was just perfect for doing what they did—Ray Berry, and Art, [and recent minority newcomers to the Eastside] and the expertise they brought. The influx, it was like a melting pot, people were from all over. They were forward-thinking people. Art was the perfect person to be president of the board at that time. He listened. That's very important because no one can have the answer to everything. We have to listen to others and consider what they have to share, in order to come up with a final decision that is in the best interest of everyone. He and Berry listened, they were a good combination. Miller, he was "staunch," he was hard nosed, he wasn't open. He wasn't flexible at all.

I am always grateful that the people who were here at the time, everybody talked, and respected each other, and the leaders who were involved at that time, they had the respect of everyone.

Over the weekend we also continued to have contact with some of the boycott leaders. A group of the leaders had called on the mayor on Saturday morning. (The mayor was not at the city-school meeting which was held at the same time.) And as late as 10:00 on Sunday night, Ray Berry met with Renfro and Bland. Ray told me the next day that it was quite clear to him that Renfro and Bland felt the whole movement was out of control. They had lost control. They wished they could direct it, but they didn't know what to do. They were hopeful that we could do something that would contain the situation.

The only feeler that we had regarding any specific proposal by the boycott leaders related to Irving School. By Monday I had received word that if we could do something for Irving School we might be able to get the boycott called off. Everybody involved was satisfied with the plan for Lowell School, but they felt that there had to be something for Irving indicating what ultimately would be done for that school.

Also on Saturday we made our first contacts with the State Department of Education. As I understood it, word had reached California Superintendent of Public Instruction Max Rafferty, from someone outside the Riverside school system. Rafferty actually placed the first call to Superintendent Miller to find out what was going on. And over the weekend there were a number of telephone calls between Riverside and Sacramento.[16] As a result, the State Department of Education agreed to send one of their best men to Riverside on Monday to see if he could be of any help to us.[17] They didn't try to impose any conditions or solutions, but they simply said they had some people who had a good deal of experience in some touchy situations and maybe they could be of help to us if we wanted.

It was at that time also that Mr. Rafferty assured Bruce Miller that if any of our applications for funds under the various programs would be of help in solving the problems they would give us a number-one priority. He was good for his word. The Riverside application for the first monies that came out of the vast federal education program, most of which is administered through the state, was the first one granted in California. We had many other pioneering kinds of applications granted from programs across the country. All of them had the strong endorsement of the State Department of Education.

Monday Morning — Washington School

School opening was Monday, September 13, 1965. I was at the administration office before school started. It was a tense time. We had done all we could do to prepare for any foreseeable eventuality. But we couldn't know how extensive the boycott might

16. From the office of Wilson Riles, a Division of Compensatory Education. Later, Mr. Riles became the first black American to become the State Superintendent of Public Instruction.

17. Theodore Neff.

Judge Charles Field: *They [the Littleworth family] did move in with us for about two or three days, Art and Evie, Anne and Todd. We had a three bedroom house, and Rob [the Field's 18 month old son] was actually still in our bedroom, so we had two open bedrooms. Evie was bubbly and energetic, a lot of fun, full of energy. She made everything a party, actually, so it was fine.*

I remember that one of the things that made Art and Evie want to move was that one of their neighbors was circulating a petition for Art's recall and there had been death threats. Evie was very uptight.

The threats were pretty vague, I don't know how they got relayed by the police, but it affected Evie a bit. I don't think they had any death threats that Art took seriously, but having your own neighbor circulating a petition for your recall bothered him. . . . And that neighbor had been a friend.

To me [the backlash against integration] started right away. I don't think the backlash ever got any legs. The meetings [of parents opposed to integration] were always emotional, not characterized by rational thought in every instance.

The toughest decision I think Art had to make was whether they were going to have an integrated school at a revived Lowell, whether they were going to bus white kids. The board basically made the decision they would not bus white kids to a school in a black neighborhood because to do so would be too divisive and it really would lead to violence, and they decided not to do that. That's not a decision, I think, that pleased all the blacks 100 percent.

The complexity was to get through the [crisis], complying with [both the letter and spirit] of the Supreme Court's ruling, and the direction society was taking, and not alienating the whites. The blacks were not unduly militant and there were a lot of responsible black leaders, but there was a chance of losing the support of the white community and that would have been a catastrophe. The board couldn't risk that. So they had to be very, very careful. The tone that was set by the school board was, "We're going to do the right thing. Period.". . . . You didn't want the school district to be at odds with a significant part of the power in the community. The community has to support the schools in an awful lot of ways, every kind of way: athletically, academically, . . . bond issues.

It was a long time ago. Riverside had one of the more dramatic experiences [with integration], dramatic in the sense that the community got together. Maybe, on balance [Lowell burning] was good. In this case, on balance, the burning did not do much harm. It did good.

You know Art had been valedictorian at Yale Law School, and he was about as bright a lawyer as you could find on the planet, and very balanced in his presentation. He was not emotional at all, just pure reason, logic. He's an amazing guy. . . . Some very balanced [black leaders] were also involved in the issue. I think that was another element, the black community was very responsible.

JUDGE CHARLES FIELD

COMMUNITY MEMBER

Charles D. Field was born in San Francisco and grew up in the Stanford, Washington D.C., and west Los Angeles areas. He was a member of the pioneer class at the University of California, Riverside, graduating with a Bachelor of Arts in 1958. He received his law degree from the University of California, Los Angeles, in 1963. From 1963 to 1990, he was a member of the Riverside law firm Best Best & Krieger, serving as senior partner in the labor and employment section and as managing partner.

He was appointed to the Riverside Superior Court in January 1990 and retired in 2004. He has served the community in many roles: as the founding chair of the UCR Foundation, as a member of the UCR Alumni Association Board of Directors, and as a member of the University of California Board of Regents where he is now regent emeritus.

Other public service roles include board member and chair of the Riverside Arts Council and board member of the Riverside County Law Library. He was elected to the board of Western Municipal Water District in 2006 and served until 2014. He was named the winner of the Frank Miller Civic Achievement Award in 2012.

be; what effect it might have; whether picket lines might be formed to prevent children who wanted to go to school from attending; if other acts of violence might occur. Mr. Neff, from the State Department of Education stopped in, but he said that he wanted to spend the day talking with the various minority leaders.

As the morning wore on, our immediate fears did not materialize, but the afternoon was still ahead of us with a School Board meeting at 4:00 p.m. There were no reports of violence or picket lines, but there was one unexpected telephone call from Washington School. It was a sit-in! This had not been planned by any of the boycott leaders, so it was a surprise to them also. Apparently it had been organized by Dr. Baugh, one of the fiery speakers at the Irving School meeting.

We learned that 54 children had arrived at Washington School who were not enrolled there but who were from the Casa Blanca school area. As we ultimately learned, some of the children were actually in an optional territory where they could have gone to Washington if there had been space and if they had made the request through normal channels.

The first problem of course was what to do with the children. We did not at that time know how widespread this might become, and of course we didn't know what was behind it. We decided that probably we should not admit the children into classes because once they were put into classes it would be very difficult to make a change. At the same time there were pretty obvious dangers in having them sit around doing nothing, or having them sent home. Some of the parents had stayed, and they were all very polite and well-mannered about it. Most of the parents, though, had simply dropped off the children and had left.

In response to the sit-in we agreed that we would dispatch several substitute teachers to Washington School, keep the children in the auditorium, and try to carry on as much schooling as we could under the circumstances. Meanwhile Ray Berry talked to those parents who had remained and tried to explain the difficulties that this situation gave us and the reasons not to put the children in classes right at that moment.

The boycott was on, but we didn't know how many children were involved. Later we learned about 250 children were gathered together in churches in the "Freedom Schools." The thing that we had feared was that there might be picket lines which would try to prevent other children from attending public schools. This did not materialize.

Monday Afternoon —
Grant School Meeting: Integration in Principle

The full Board had lunch together on Monday before the formal School Board meeting was to begin at four o'clock. Today we could not do that because of the Brown Act. The Brown Act requires all meetings of officials be open to the public, with narrow exceptions. Today, meetings have to be posted with time and place noted, with notice to the press. And the public officials must have an agenda for their meetings, and with strict exceptions, they cannot take up any matter not on the agenda. But in 1965, closed meetings to handle emergency situations were accepted without restriction.

In this crisis, informal meetings were invaluable to the Board. They gave us an opportunity to discuss what might come up from a hostile audience and what I could say with the full support of the Board. As president of the Board I would chair the meeting, and I was determined there would be no repetition of Friday's volatile rally at Irving School. As president I was expected to respond to the questions and comments from the audience. To some of the minority community I was the "headman" with the power to make all decisions right then and there. And when I didn't do that, we were perceived as being evasive and putting them off. They wanted answers, even negative answers. If I were to speak for the whole school system, it was imperative that I had the Board and administration behind me.

We discussed the whole problem at lunch but specifically whether or not there was anything we could say at the Board meeting with respect to Irving School. We also discussed the question of whether I could commit to a belief in the principle of integration. The Board was no stranger to the subject of integration. We and the minority community had considered it in 1961 and again in 1963. Our Open Enrollment policy had existed since 1961, and the Board's commitment in 1963 was to upgrade the minority neighborhood schools. The Board—with the support of the minority community—had rejected integration in favor of their neighborhood schools. Now, two years later, the situation had changed. The African-American community apparently wanted integration—without delay.

We decided two things: one, that Lowell School would be closed, and that we would make a beginning of integration at Irving School, probably with the kindergarten. And two, that I could say that the Board was committed to the principle of integration, and that this would be a foundation of the 30-day study which had been requested.

In the afternoon Mr. Neff came back with very discouraging results. He said that he didn't think he had been able to accomplish anything all day. He had been talking with a number of people, and, as he saw it, it was probably impossible for us to head off violence. At that point I asked the superintendent to call the chief of police and to have plainclothes policemen at the Board meeting at Grant School at 4 p.m.

The Board meeting had been changed to the auditorium at Grant because of the expected large audience. The auditorium was packed, but orderly with both minorities and whites present. We began the meeting with the report by the superintendent setting forth the Lowell plan as it had been developed. Transfer approximately 239 children from Lowell's kindergarten to third grade to seven different schools with low minority enrollments and transfer at least the kindergarten students and perhaps some students from grades one and two from Irving School. Transportation would be provided. Lowell School was to be closed within three years. This plan was formally adopted by the Board.

Then I made some introductory remarks in which I set forth our determination to make a beginning of integration at Irving School and also our commitment "to the full integration" of all Riverside schools. After that I opened the meeting for questions, discussion, and comments.

Some of the people, both black and white, spoke in favor of integration. Some spoke of the litany of broken promises. Some comments were hostile, nasty, and carried with them totally unjust accusations against the schools. Some people said we were giving in to the threat of force. As a lawyer, I had handled some unruly and raucous crowds, and I had concluded that the best way of dealing with public comment, even with outrageous speakers, was to let them say whatever they wanted without restrictions by rules of procedure. Some governmental agencies make people fill out cards before they can speak. Some require the questions be put in writing. Some require a time limit, frequently two or three minutes per speaker. Many government agencies do not respond to the people's comments, there is no dialogue. I did none of these. I merely called on people who raised their hands—and I answered them in as calm a voice and as factually as possible. I had learned a long time before to be cool under pressure. And this is what I did at the Grant School meeting.

There was one question during the latter part of the meeting which raised a legitimate but potentially explosive subject, a subject I had been dreading. A black mother said, "You are going to bus black children around, why not bus white children too?" I took a hitch in my belt and decided that a straight answer was deserved, even though it could blow up the meeting. I answered her, "You have a chance to improve the education of your children, without affecting the white children. But Riverside won't accept busing white children to achieve integration. The Board would be voted out of office." Whether that decision was right or wrong, it was a practical answer. I waited for a reaction. There was none.

After that exchange, the tone of the meeting was considerably more constructive. There was no one saying that the boycott would be called off, but there was hope. The meeting lasted about three hours and ended with an orderly adjournment.

After the Board meeting most of the black people adjourned to the Masonic Hall on the Eastside. The debate was whether or not the boycott should be called off. The local people by-and-large felt that enough had been accomplished and that they should end the boycott. However, the non-Riversiders still wanted to fight. A vote was

The Press, *Tuesday, September 14, 1965, with an article showing students attending Freedom School classes.*

ONE-DAY BOYCOTT — Carrying sign (above) was L. E. Leer an Eastside resident who said he had no connection with the boycott group but agreed with their aims. Leer had three signs which he alternated carrying at Irving School yesterday. Rod Fielder, teacher, listens (center photo) to Johnny Bennet, 10, read aloud to get some idea of his reading level in a "freedom school" fifth grade class at a Masonic hall at 12th near Park. Kindergarten students at the "freedom school" at 12th near Park enjoy (right photo) their first mid-morning "milk break" during the first day of operation of the school by parents boycotting Lowell and Irving schools. The youngsters were served bread and jelly with their milk. Their morale was said to be high.   (Staff photos by Bob Ringquist)

THE MUSIC MAN — Kindergarten pupils in a freedom school class yesterday have a sing-along.   (Staff photo by Bob Ringquist)

Opening day
Most pupils like 'Freedom School'

By JOHN MONTGOMERY

Some 100 grade school children — the majority of whom attended Lowell and Irving schools in Riverside last year — quietly went school yesterday in two eastside churches. The sites were among the six where freedom schools were conducted yesterday.

AME CHURCH, 10th and Sedgewick, was school for 30 fourth graders, 20 boys and 10 girls, and the Amos Temple CME Church, 11th and Victoria, opened its doors to 40 first-graders and 30 second graders.

Mrs. Sarah Seekins, one of the three teachers at the school set up in the AME Church, and a senior at University of California, Riverside, said:

"I read in the Daily Press that teachers were needed so I just volunteered. I hope to stay as long as I'm needed but I'm supposed to be back to classes at college next Monday."

MOST OF HER fourth-grade pupils were formerly at Lowell and Irving. Mrs.

✔ Dennis Allison, 10, 4475 Grove, an Irving student last year — "I liked it better in Los Angeles. I was visiting there during the riots — but I didn't get in them."

✔ Daryl Jones, 10½, of 2810 10th — "It's all right. I liked it a little better at Irving. But I live just down the street from here and can go home for lunch. Most of the kids have to bring their lunch."

MRS. SEEKINS said that although some of the chil-

dren brought their own lunch, sandwiches and punch were provided by the school headquarters set up in the Masonic Auditorium.

At the Amos Temple, classrooms were set up for 30 second-graders, and some 40 first graders, Mrs. Margaret Past and Mrs. Ernest Heeren are in charge of the first graders.

"These children are very well behaved," remarked Mrs. Past. "They get along very nicely. We've had them

playing games and telling about what they did this summer."

A SUBSTITUTE teacher in charge of the second-graders said: "These children all know they are here because of the boycott at Lowell and Irving. But they all behave beautifully. I've never seen children behave better."

In the second-grade class, 28 attended Lowell last year, 5 were from Irving, 1 from Victoria, and 1 from a school in another community.

Plenty of action on tap at Los Angeles County Fair

With the accent on action, the Los Angeles County Fair opens Friday at Pomona, and 17 days of special events and plenty of action to the world's largest county fair.

And there are 40,000 exhibits to see.

Free action will include grandstand entertainment, the

ing and aquatic sports are demonstrated daily, are other fair attractions that have proved popular in past years.

WITH 40,000 exhibits to choose from, there is a bit of everything to see.

The Flower and Garden Show features florists' ar-

Fair visitors can tour the 350-foot tunnels and see an early-day mine office. Original equipment from a Grass Valley mine also will be displayed.

AND THERE'S still more to be seen.

Table settings, weaving

Max Rafferty, California Superintendent of Public Instruction from 1963 to 1971.

Wilson Riles, head of the Division of Compensatory Education and later California Superintendent of Public Instruction from 1971 to 1982.

Theodore Neff, shown in 2014, was the state representative sent to Riverside by Max Rafferty and Wilson Riles.

Photo by Sue Cockerell, Davis Enterprise.

71

held, and the result was in favor of calling off the boycott. I'm not sure of the truth of this, but it is a humorous twist if it is true. (No newspaper reporters were present; I understand they were asked to leave that meeting.) But apparently, from what I've been told, the CORE people refused to accept the vote. They began storming around, trying a number of procedural maneuvers to get the vote reconsidered. Just then a very practical politician turned off the lights. It was about 11:00 p.m. and when they finally got the lights turned back on, most of the people had gone home.

That was the end of the boycott.

The Community-at-Large Reaction

When the School Board determined that it had thirty days to develop a plan for integration, the general public was aroused. For a period after the first day of school and the Monday Board meeting, I and my family continued to receive police protection, and although I have no specific memory of personal threats, my daughter remembers our discovery one morning of a cross that had been burned on the lawn of our home during the ongoing crisis.

My telephone numbers and address were listed in the telephone directory, and I received a huge number of phone calls and letters. My phone was usually busy from the time I got home at night until after bedtime. I tried to answer most of the calls responsibly. Sometimes I really couldn't talk about it anymore, and in this era before answering machines, my wife, Evie, would take the call. Most of the calls and letters came from average people, not those who were part of the power structure in Riverside.

Many were supportive of what the Board had done. A few callers, (probably three or four) said flatly that they did not want their children to associate with black children. And if integration was going to cause that, they would remove their children to a private school or move out of town. I did not receive any calls or letters with any pressure from the "establishment" saying that if you don't keep those blacks in their place you'll get no more law business. However, I did receive a surprising number of letters from people in high governmental positions and leading businessmen who said they were much impressed by what was going on, and they thought we were doing the right thing. One of these was Ivan Hinderaker, the chancellor of the University of California at Riverside. This led to a close personal friendship and a good working relationship between the Riverside school system and UCR.[18]

Most of the calls or letters were concerned with what integration could accomplish in a way that would not degrade the standards for the other children. They didn't mind if some African-American children were transferred to the "receiving" schools, but they were adamantly against having their own children taken out of their neighborhood schools and sent to Irving, Lowell, and Casa Blanca. I received more telephone calls and letters in support of what we were trying to do than opposed, which was a little surprising to me.

18. Irving H. Balow, the head of UCR's education department, was later appointed to the Riverside School Board, and numerous programs were organized between the Riverside schools and UCR.

DELL ROBERTS
PARENT, COACH, ADMINISTRATOR

Dell Roberts is a community leader in the Eastside. He went to Longfellow School and then to Riverside Polytechnic High School, where he was an All Citrus Belt League guard in football and lettered in swimming, football, and track.

While still in elementary school, he went to work at Butcher Boy, a local food processor, owned by the Roberts family, whose son, Duane Roberts, went on to own the Mission Inn. Dell did clean-up and helped to unload trucks. He also worked picking fruit and cutting lawns until he spotted an opportunity as a lifeguard at Lincoln Park pool.

After graduation from Riverside Polytechnic High School, he worked at Butcher Boy full time at night, supervising the unloading of trucks, cutting meat, and supervising hamburger meat crews. In 1965, he began working for Poly High School during the day, becoming a campus supervisor and coach.

His ability to promote teamwork, self-confidence, and student safety led to a position in the school's administration. He became assistant principal in charge of discipline and ran his office with student labor answering phones, receiving people, writing and delivering passes, and gaining real world experience. In 1990, he went to work in the district offices as administrative assistant for campus and community services until he retired in 2003.

Dell Roberts: It was a very restive time for black students. They had hired me because I had some sort of rapport with the students. In fact, when I wrote a guide for campus supervisors on campus violence, [a point I made] was that the first thing you should do, when there's a problem, is release your coaches, put your coaches in the middle of frays. Coaches have that command of students which English teachers and math teachers don't have. A coach can walk into the middle of a crowd and holler, "Hey Jim," and the [students] respond.

My first two sons, in fact, probably the third too, went to Lowell. The problem with Lowell was that we didn't like the fact that it had become de facto *segregated, the fact we didn't feel [the students] were getting an equal education.*

I remember going and supporting [Art] with my presence at the many meetings, like the one they had at Irving School in the auditorium [September 10th], where he was just getting lambasted by everybody over the integration situation. They were rough. I thought, "Here is this lone white man sitting up there taking all kinds of verbal abuse because they weren't happy with the process."

They were trying to upset him, and had he gotten upset, it would have been counterproductive. He was just calm, and I always admired him. It was just great that he could do that. It was just Art, sitting on that stage. I was a little bit fearful for him but really respectful of him.

One meeting I went to, I did not speak. I wanted to hear people's positions and not really speak to anything. When I left, about three or four people came out with me and said, "Dell Roberts, we stayed an extra half an hour to hear you speak and you didn't say anything." I said, "I'm sorry, I didn't come to speak, I came to listen so that I would know in my mind exactly where people on the board stood."

My three sons were bused to Pachappa. At the crest of the issue, I thought that was a good thing but in retrospect, it wasn't that good, for them. I went over to the school. What I found out was that, in at least some of the classes, the teachers were teaching around them because they didn't think they had the capability. I went to one classroom and soon as I stepped in, the tempo rose in the room with kids starting to talk and throw things. The teacher walked up to me apologetically and said, "Those are the bus kids." . . . Yes.

So I was very disheartened, told her thank you, and I went to the office and had my child immediately removed from her class.

The Riverside City Council took the position that the issue was the schools' problem and not the city's in general. Councilman John Sotelo tried unsuccessfully to get a resolution adopted by the city council in support of the School Board. Nevertheless, Mayor Lewis was vocal in his support. *The Press-Enterprise*, which had covered the crisis most carefully and thoroughly, also came out in favor for integration.

During this 30-day period I spoke to many groups, some that you might normally expect to be fairly conservative. I remember one group in particular—the Downtown Lions Club. The Club turned out to be very understanding of the problems we faced. I realized that we couldn't convince everybody, but at least people understood that the School Board faced extremely difficult decisions. We had been decisive, and had not closed our eyes to problems that might grow more serious in the future. The fire at Lowell School, and the fires during the Los Angeles riots just a few weeks earlier, were unspoken but very much in the minds of many.

I summed up my presentation to the Lions Club this way—my constant refrain in many meetings: "We have an opportunity to benefit the education of minority children. It will not be at the expense of your children. We headed off a racial crisis. Give us a chance to make the program work."

The warm reception I had received at the Lions Club (I was a Kiwanian) was about to be offset by a potentially hostile group of white parents. We heard about a group that was going to oppose the Board, and there were rumors about my recall. But I was invited to "simply explain what was going on." About 50 people gathered in the conference room of an investment house in the Magnolia Center area. I was told that there were two or three representatives from each school in the city and they were obviously not in sympathy with what had been done. It was just a question of how much opposition there might be.

As I started to speak, I noticed that Bland and Renfro had slipped into the back of the room. In order to avoid future embarrassment I referenced them in my remarks. Mrs. Holmes, who had invited me, interrupted the meeting to introduce them, and she asked if they wouldn't come up and answer questions along with me. Mr. Bland finally did, and we made a surprisingly effective pair answering questions in what turned out to be a long night.

At the end, a gentleman, a Mr. Conde as I recall, asked if he could say something. He spoke eloquently on what the African American was trying to do. He went through the black problems—unemployment, crime rates, and all of the things with which we are familiar. He said, "Those of us who are trying to help, ask ourselves, where do we start? It seemed," he said, "that the best place to start is with education. What we want to do is to try to educate our children the best way we can so that we will improve the lot of our own people and try to solve the problems that America is

WALTER PARKS
SCHOOL DISTRICT CONTROLLER

In 1965, Walter Parks was Controller for the school district under Harry K. Young, the assistant superintendent for business. A graduate with an MBA from Stanford University, he started with the school district in 1962, and succeeded Mr. Young in 1968. He ended his career with the district in 1983, retiring to start a second career in business, forming a portable classroom leasing company.

In 1986, he became the third president of the Mission Inn Foundation, during the crucial period of the building's renovation. He was a member of the first docent class and led the first docent tour when the Inn reopened in 1993. He is the author of *The Famous Fliers' Wall of the Mission Inn* (1986). He lectures on the Mata Ortiz ceramic art movement and is the author of *The Miracle of Mata Ortiz* (Rio Nuevo Publishers, 2011).

Walter Parks: *Dick Purviance was one of the best principals in the district. He could see that the children under Compensatory Education were not measuring up educationally to the rest of the district but he thought the concept of the neighborhood school was very important.*

For Ray Berry, it wasn't a matter of social policy but of educational opportunities for all students. He truly believed that. Ray was a theorist to a certain degree. He believed that, if given the opportunity, these [minority] children would flourish alongside a lot of other achieving students, that being [in the same classrooms] would take the lid off and allow them to blossom. He was really the author of the integration plan.

Before the board dealt with integration, school board meetings were very casual affairs, with about 20 to 25 people in the room including the press, representatives of the PTA, the board, of course, and administrative staff. We all sat around a big horseshoe table and there was an amount of informal chitchat and conversation. After, the meetings became very formal. The board was seated on a stage with the staff below. There was a microphone set up for people to address the board. It was significantly different.

Bruce Miller was a big gregarious man who knew everybody, and during the course of integration, he really became marginalized. The black leadership didn't really trust anybody, but they did trust Ray Berry. Bruce Miller represented authority, he represented decades of unfulfilled promises. He'd made sincere efforts but he didn't understand the depth of resentment some people felt. And those people were now vocal. In fact, many people I knew didn't understand what was going on.

Bruce Miller wasn't the only one. The administration was generally old line and very comfortable with that. They saw a lot of the new challenges of integration as disrespect of authority, and they just didn't make it as things changed.

The [leaders in the community] trusted Ray because he was quiet and had a calm demeanor. That was his leadership technique, and he put together a real team. The personnel director, the director of special education, the director of education, he listened to everything they said, then in the end, after he had heard everyone, he'd say, "I think we should do this. . ."

He had some very interesting ideas about education and he wanted to get them out. He wrote very well. He saw not only the challenges of desegregation but also changes in the district itself, areas of rapid growth and areas of declining enrollment, great geographical imbalances. He led us through that. He was a very fine leader in his quiet style.

Ray had the trust of many people, and when radical things began to happen, the burning of the Lowell School and the Freedom School, the leadership in the community felt they could work with Ray and trust what he said.

. . . Parks continued on page 77

facing now." It was extremely well done, and I don't think anyone could have said anything better. It was exactly the right note to end on with a potentially hostile audience. He received a good deal of applause. We will never know exactly, but that meeting probably headed off the development of a strong anti-integration group. It seemed to take the fire out of the opposition.

The Integration Pledge

At the close of the Grant School meeting on September 13, 1965, the Board directed the administration to prepare a comprehensive plan for integration by the second Board meeting on the 18th of October. This was in keeping with the pledge I had made at the Irving School meeting, that in thirty days we would have developed an integration plan if the boycott was called off. I was determined to keep that promise. It was essential not to give the minority community any reason to doubt us.

Still, thirty days was a short time for a public agency to produce a plan. We had no precedents for a voluntary integration effort. There was little written about it, how to best accomplish it, or what the effects might be. What we were planning to do was well in advance of the 1967 Coleman Report, "Racial Isolation in the Public Schools." This was a massive report commissioned by the U.S. government that would conclude that socially disadvantaged black children benefitted significantly from learning in mixed-race classrooms.

Integration, it seemed to me, could be justified on a common sense basis without any scholarly reports. I had talked with many teachers who worked with minority children and they told me that they believed integration would bring about improvement in the education of these children.

Dave Foley, the principal of Gage Junior High, told me that it was hard to get Casa Blanca students to be part of Gage. They felt left out before they even got to junior high. The girls were timid; the boys were sometimes aggressive. A simple example also comes out of the Casa Blanca situation. In Casa Blanca there were a percentage of families where no English, or virtually no English, was spoken at home. The children came to school with a severe English handicap. They were exposed to "good" English only from the teacher in the classroom. They didn't hear it on the playground; they didn't hear it at recess; they didn't hear it during lunch; they didn't hear it before or after school; and they didn't hear it at home. The teacher was up against overwhelming odds. When a student's language skills are not good, it affects reading, writing, and all other subjects. The same problems existed in certain black families in segregated schools—the use of "black" English, limited vocabulary, and grammar particular to that slang.

Parks continued from page 75

I remember the meeting [at Grant School] on September 13th, Monday at 4 p.m. Robert Bland was very challenging, almost accusing, not appreciating the Board's position. Also Jess Carlos and Jess Ybarra. But by this time it was almost [an anticlimax]. The board voted for integration but Art Littleworth made it clear that this was a significant change and you couldn't expect a change like that overnight. He asked for thirty days and said, "We'll have a plan."

The plan was presented at Magnolia School Auditorium [October 18th]. I remember seeing Art at the front; Robert Bland was standing to the left of me. The crisis was over in that moment.

The ability of the district to be consistent, over time, in managing the desegregation was important. Everyone realized that de facto segregation was wrong but they had to figure out a way to desegregate without shredding the district. What I saw was the effort, a genuine effort, to recognize that the needs of the minority community were not the same as the needs of the majority community and to make up for whatever deficiencies had occurred for those students.

The major change was the introduction of individualized education. It was Ray Berry that thought it through; he set up a district-wide program and a team based on meeting the individual needs of each child.

Above: Grant School, the site of the meeting on September 13, 1965, where the board committed to desegregate Riverside schools.

While teachers said there were educational benefits to integration, I believed that social advantages were the more important benefits in Riverside. We had a chance to do something that would bring the community together as one, that we were one people and one community. We had an opportunity to send a message that the complaints of the minority community were going to be listened to carefully, and we were going to try to do something about them. We had to build some trust in the school system and in government in general.

We had the opportunity to build hope in the minority community, along with the rest of Riverside, for a better life. Out of the crisis we were in, that was my primary goal.

Left to right, starting with the back row: Riverside Unified School District 1965 Board of Education and Superintendent—Vernon Stern, B. Rae Sharp, Bruce Miller (superintendent), Evelyn Kendrick, Arthur Littleworth (president), and Margaret Heers.

CHAPTER 6 — THE INTEGRATION PLAN

The 30-Day Period

There was no question that the School Board and the administration by themselves had to develop the integration plan. It was their responsibility. Besides there was no time to hire a consultant or an expert. The Board did organize a small advisory committee, but its function was simply to react to the proposals submitted by the school system, not to generate a plan itself. I called it the "sounding board" committee, as it would also help us to gauge our community's reaction. Each of the committee members had a widespread following. We appointed African Americans; Mexican Americans, including residents from Casa Blanca and the Eastside; and white parents, teachers, and businessmen.

The members of the Advisory Committee for Integrated Schools were: Percy Baugh, M.D., Robert Bland, Mrs. Richard Boylan, Jr., Jesse Carlos, William H. Davis, Augustine A. Flores, Mrs. Maxine Frost, Truman Johnson, Mrs. Patricia Kennington, Joseph Palaia, Donald E. Renfro, Mrs. Belen Reyes, and Richard Roa. Also included as members were Board members Heers and Kendrick and myself and administrators Miller and Berry. Truman Johnson, President of Citrus Belt Savings and Loan Association, appointed as the one "conservative" member, turned out to be one of the most vocal in support of integration. Maxine Frost was later appointed to the School Board and served some thirty years until her death. During all that time she remained a champion of integration.

Initially there were various options for the plan. What to do about Casa Blanca? The majority of parents in Casa Blanca liked their neighborhood school just the way it was. Should Irving be closed? Or should we be sending white children to Irving, since the school had been rebuilt just ten years before? Should the parents have the choice of integrating or not? Should integration be implemented in stages? How long should it take? At first, the only sure thing about the plan was that Lowell should be closed and not be rebuilt.

There were certain logistical matters about which more information was needed before any plan could be developed. To that end Superintendent Miller launched a full-scale assault by mobilizing his staff: Dr. Donald Taylor, assistant to the superintendent and one of the strongest supporters of integration, was assigned to determine what the district would need in the way of school housing. Walter Parks, the controller, submitted data on the costs of additional housing and transportation. Paul Lockhart, director of transportation, was in charge of arrangements for busing. Harry Young, assistant superintendent for business, had the task of relocating the district's portable classrooms. And Ray Berry and Assistant Superintendent of Pupil Personnel Services Dr. Richard Robbins were assigned to determine how many reading specialists, counselors, aides, and tutors were needed to insure the success of the plan. Successful integration, it was certain, would require more than mere desegregation.

The combined administration effort, however, showed that integration could be accomplished in fairly short order and at reasonable costs.

The initial plans from the administration were at a slower pace than finally adopted, and at first they gave the parents the freedom of choice of integrating or not. Both the Board and administration were opposed to "cross-busing," that is, transporting white children into Irving or Casa Blanca. I felt it might seriously jeopardize the entire plan and said so. My goal was to develop an integration plan without splitting the Riverside community the way cross-busing had done in Syracuse, New York.

Then, one day during the planning month, I came into the administration office and Ray Berry announced that he had come to the conclusion that all minority children should be integrated whether their parents believed in it or not. His contacts with minority teachers and teachers who taught minority students had led him to that conclusion. The educators felt that there was only one real answer to the problems of minority children, and that was complete integration. Berry and the staff believed that integration would be good for the community and good for the children.

This was a dramatic change in course. To Casa Blanca this meant more than just the integration of a school. What was really at stake was whether Casa Blanca should continue to remain a small Mexican-American community that happened to be in Riverside but wasn't really a part of it, or whether the people there should become full-fledged Riverside participants.

The significance of Berry's conclusion took time to settle in with the Board, the administration, and the Advisory Committee for Integrated Schools. That committee was asked originally to consider, among other duties, whether integration should be mandated in total or whether some freedom of choice would be permissible. Although some appointments to the Advisory Committee were thought to be "conservative," all of the members turned out to be in favor of integration.

But now, however, the committee was faced with a petition signed by the parents of 300 of the 370 children enrolled at Casa Blanca demanding that Casa Blanca School not be closed, and that the students "not be bused out except on an optional basis." There were spirited discussions, but in the end the committee's decisions were unanimous: that a broadly based committee of Casa Blanca area representatives of major interests and parents, called the Casa Blanca Study Committee, be established to study how best to "completely integrate the pupils of Casa Blanca"; that unless the Study Committee had a "better plan," Casa Blanca School boundaries would be changed so that one-third of the pupils would be transferred to Washington School; and that transportation would be provided for all wishing to transfer to other schools in which the racial balance would allow additional minority pupils. Today, with no school in Casa Blanca, children attend seven different elementary schools.

The School Board, the administration, and the Advisory Committee were all united in the integration plan that would be presented on October 18th.

The Master Plan of School Integration

The Plan for Integration was presented at an evening meeting on October 18th at the Magnolia School auditorium. The auditorium was packed. The audience was split: fifty percent were in favor of the plan (whites and blacks), and fifty percent—mostly whites—opposed.

The minority community, which included several members of our Advisory Committee, demanded that it be voted on that evening. They were afraid that opposition would develop and the Board would weaken. I refused to hold a vote. While the general parts of the integration plan were known to some, I thought the public at large deserved to see the plan in total before the vote was taken. I set October 25, 1965, one week later, for an additional hearing and a vote.

The plan was a one-page document that specified six basic actions:

Lowell. Close the school in September 1966. Change the school boundary so that approximately one hundred children would be transferred across Tequesquite Arroyo to Alcott School. The rest of the children would be transported by bus to other low-minority "receiving" schools.

Irving. Close the school in 1966. All of the children would be transported by bus to other low-minority "receiving" schools. The buildings at Irving would be used for Head Start classes, a district-wide reading clinic, adult education, and other programs. [Irving was finally used for Lincoln, the continuation high school.]

Emerson. In February 1966, change the school boundary so that approximately 126 children would be transferred to Highland and Hyatt Schools. [Emerson had about a fifty percent minority enrollment at the time.]

Casa Blanca. Appoint a representative citizens' committee to study the Casa Blanca situation and report in May 1966. Unless the committee came up with a better plan, boundary change and busing would begin in 1966 and 1967. [The citizens' committee voted to close the school in 1967, and this was approved by the School Board. The Casa Blanca buildings were eventually transferred to the City of Riverside to become a community center.]

Transitional Education. This became the new word for "Compensatory Education." It was to provide transitional and enrichment programs where needed in the District as a whole. This included teacher aides, tutors, remedial reading classes, counseling, smaller classes, and libraries where possible. It would continue progress in curriculum development aiming toward broad, flexible programming in all areas. It included encouraging participation in adult education, broadening research into dropout rates and vocational education, and applying the results to curriculum development. The Board would apply for federal funds to cover the cost of special programs.

Segregation. Housing patterns could result in the development of other segregated schools, and boundary changes and other adjustments would be made as needed to prevent such development. [In 1968 boundary changes were made in the junior high schools to prevent segregation. University Heights Junior High School was closed and the property was transferred to the city as Bobby Bonds Sports Complex and community center.]

Wanda [Poole] Scruggs: *I come from a family of six girls, three older girls and three younger girls. I was part of the three older girls. We attended Lowell School from kindergarten until it was fire bombed in 1965. My twin sister and I were both in Mrs. Doskocil's class. When Lowell was firebombed, we then attended Freedom School over at Lincoln Park. [Afterward], my sister and I both went to Pachappa.*

My father had six girls, and he told us we were all princesses. So we went to [the new] school like [we were making an entry], "Okay. We're here."

We were very, very confident, very self-assured. We weren't demure or timid in the least. And we were heads and shoulders taller than anybody in the class, so everybody had to look up to us.

It helped tremendously. I remember even going into my fifth grade class with Mrs. Watt at Pachappa School. I walked in and said, "Hi Teach, how're you?"

She said, "Don't call me Teach, again." We were really very confident.

And having participated in the Freedom School, I think that made us feel more like celebrities. Because the news came, some news truck came, and put us on the news that day, put us in the newspaper. So we kind of felt like celebrities. So there wasn't much people could tell us to make us feel bad about being black, for one thing, or being transferred to a new school. I think it was kind of evident with almost all of the kids [that transferred], "All right, we are the celebrities. You guys don't have as much notoriety as we do." We didn't really feel like [we] were victimized, we were celebrities.

Because Sandra and I were twins and we were very, very tall, there weren't that many kids that messed with us. I remember my sixth grade teacher, Mrs. Lyman, she was a wonderful teacher, and she used to just pull me, now and then, to the side and say, "Wanda, I just think you are a special kid."

I used to say, "Well, thank you." I always took it positively. I don't know what her intention was, negative or positive. But, she always said, "Wanda, you're a special kid." Because we excelled academically, we were good students, we were athletic. We just did a lot of things, we always participated.

My daddy always subscribed to the Daily Enterprise *and I remember seeing [my father's name] in a column protesting segregation, in a letter to the editor. He was very vocal. The parents were privy to the information [academic records and student achievement comparisons], that there was a difference, a marked difference. One thing I do remember, moving to Pachappa School exposed us to more Caucasians than we had ever seen before, but in being exposed, it helped us to learn how to deal with Caucasians, it helped us in terms of knowing how to better communicate with them. Because had we been thrown into that environment a little later on, we might not have been as comfortable.*

WANDA [POOLE] SCRUGGS

STUDENT AT LOWELL SCHOOL

Wanda [Poole] Scruggs grew up in the Eastside and with her sisters attended Lowell School. Her favorite teacher was Mrs. Doskocil [Doris Haddy] and she was in the same fourth grade class with Denise Matthews and Craig Goodwin.

Her family moved to Rubidoux and she graduated from Rubidoux High School and went on to graduate in Liberal Studies at California Baptist University. Wanda started her career at the University of California, Riverside, at the University Extension Center in 1986 and then moved to the office of the vice chancellor for advancement. In 2005 she joined the development team and served in various capacities including major gifts qualification officer, director of special gifts, and director of development for the university libraries. She recently retired from UCR and is now a realtor with Exit Twin Advantage Realty in Murrieta.

Wanda and Denise organized a Lowell School reunion in 2009.

...Scruggs continued on page 85

In all, about 1,000 children would be moved in 1966. The classroom-by-classroom approach in the receiving schools would mean true integration, only about five minority pupils in each classroom, rather than moving groups of children who would then just be segregated in a new location. Nineteen additional classrooms would be needed at the receiving schools. Six would have to be newly built; the remaining classrooms would be portables already owned by the District and moved to the appropriate locations. The cost of additional classrooms would be mostly offset by the fire insurance proceeds for Lowell School and the sale of the property at Lowell. After the classroom shifting was completed, no receiving school was expected to have fewer than 8 percent or more than 18 percent minority students. The cost of busing, approximately $45,000 per year, would be reimbursed by the federal government.

Approval of the Integration Plan

The October 18th Meeting

About thirty speakers were heard at the Magnolia School meeting on October 18th, both in favor and against the plan. The meeting was orderly and less passionate than the earlier meetings.

The opposition centered around the boycott and the pressure that the Board faced, the Board's hasty response, the lack of community involvement, the costs of the plan, and the fact that recently constructed school buildings were going to be empty.

The proponents of the plan stressed the fact that it was the right thing to do and that the minority pupils and the community would be better off with integration. Mayor Ben Lewis strongly supported the plan, although the Riverside City Council remained uncommitted. The following organizations indicated support: *The Press-Enterprise*; John Secor, executive secretary of the Riverside Teachers Association speaking individually; Rev. Max Ullon, president of the Riverside Human Relations Council; the American G.I. Forum; the University District Democratic Club; John Torchia, president of the local AFL-CIO; and Kenneth Wood, the Alcott principal.

Those opposed to the plan, mostly white parents from the Alcott area, had one week to organize, and they put together an impressive petition drive in that time.

The October 25th Meeting

About 500 people were jammed into the Magnolia School auditorium on October 25th. This was a special meeting of the School Board, and I was chairman. In the week after the integration plan was first presented on October 18th, the white protestors to the plan were able to collect some 1,600 signatures on two petitions which they submitted at this meeting. They had found the present plan to be "unacceptable," and demanded that the Board postpone action for a year until "a

Scruggs continued from page 83

[We] realized that sometimes there are some good ones and bad ones, just like there are in every race. I think it was beneficial to a certain extent because it helped us to learn how to get along with everybody, not just the minorities that we were used to. It kind of threw us out of our comfort zone.

In terms of later on in life, I still feel that it was beneficial for us. I really do, in that it helped us to know how to interact and to deal with people of all colors, all genders, all races. It helped us to become more sensitive to people in general, more compassionate, because we'd been through some things, and we had experienced a little racism, in terms of when we first got to Pachappa. People had, a little, called us names, but we didn't internalize it. We just kind of said, "We're not ignorant, you are, because you don't know who we really are." So, it wasn't really something that affected us and had a long lasting negative impact.

On the flip side, it was more of a positive impact, because it reinforced that not only were we valuable human beings but we didn't stoop to name calling and things like that. I think that's what that whole experience did, it really reaffirmed the things my daddy told us . . . a sense of pride in who you are. We still have it to this day. We are all graduates from college, all six of us. Even my daughters, I have four daughters and three of four have all graduated from college.

Below: Teacher Doris [Doskocil] Haddy's 1964–1965 fourth grade class, Lowell School. Three of the students are interviewed in this book: Wanda [Poole] Scruggs second from the right, second row from the bottom; Denise Matthews, top row, third from left; and Craig Goodwin, second from left, second row from the bottom.

more comprehensive plan can be presented to the electorate." The second petition called for no busing and no closing of schools.

The opponents' case for a delay in our decision and no busing was presented by a young naval officer. It was respectful, reasoned, and forceful. There were other orderly speakers, more opposed to the plan than in favor of it.

After the last speaker was heard, I turned to the individual Board members to speak: B. Rae Sharp, the vice president of the Board, and a leading accountant in Riverside; Dr. Vernon M. Stern, a professor at UCR; Evelyn H. Kendrick; and Margaret B. Heers, both mothers of children in our school system and long associated with school activities. The Board members were extremely capable, were respectful of the views of the other Board members, and were entirely dedicated to the Riverside school system. They had no political agenda except the betterment of the schools. They were unpaid and did not view their positions as a stepping-stone for the next political appointment or election. They each took a few minutes to say that he or she supported the integration plan. This was a moment of high drama.

As for myself, I answered specifically the critics of the plan. The opponents' request for a delay did not deal with the severe racial crisis. And, moreover, we were not going to know anything more in a year that we knew right then. Further, the plea for no busing was ironic. Short of continuing Riverside's *de facto* segregated schools, the only way to protect the established white schools was to close the segregated schools and bus those children to receiving integrated schools. If the segregated schools were to continue, there probably would be federal court intervention which might force white students to be bused to the segregated schools in order to achieve racial balance. In fact, later in 1968, the federal court ordered "cross-busing" to eliminate segregation in the Pasadena schools. As a result, parents in the upper and middle classes in Pasadena pulled their children from integrated public schools and placed them in private schools. In 2004, Pasadena had 63 private schools; the proportion of white students in the public schools had fallen 16 percent.

In conclusion, I acknowledged the wrongs that had been done to the African Americans. I said that while certainly the schools had begun to address minority education problems, I felt we could do more, and we should do more. The integration plan would offer a chance for a better education and hope for a better life. What was presented was a workable plan, and I felt it had the broad support of the community. It was the right thing to do.

The Board vote for the integration plan was unanimous.

We learned that the white parents who opposed the plan had a separate meeting later that evening. There was talk about a recall of School Board members and a

SUE STRICKLAND

TEACHER AT EMERSON AND HIGHLAND SCHOOLS

Sue Strickland was born in Riverside and went to Irving School. She went on to Los Angeles City College, then to California State University, Los Angeles. She is a retired teacher who started her career in Bloomington.

Sue met her husband, Reggie, in the Eastside, where he also attended Irving School and lived with his grandmother for a few years before moving to San Bernardino. Sue and Reggie reconnected again at California State University, Los Angeles and after they married, they went to Tacoma, Washington. Sue and Reggie were married 57 years until Reggie's death in 2014.

From 1958 through 1961, Sue was in Riverside teaching at Jefferson School. In 1961, the family moved to Los Angeles, then returned again for the 1964 school year and she taught at Emerson School. In February 1966, Sue was selected to transfer with Emerson students to Highland School as a part of the integration plan.

Sue is a long time volunteer for the Riverside African American Historical Society.

Sue Strickland: *Those meetings were something, too. There were some interesting meetings. Riverside always prides itself on being the first in the nation to voluntarily desegregate, but they always leave out, "after our school was burned." That's kind of a key point. Recently, I was in a meeting with some people here in Riverside and I said, "That was after the school was burned," and they said, "You had a school burn?" They didn't know.*

My mother lived across the street from the school. And she would have all these meetings. Then the night when Lowell burned, she called me and said, "Sue, they burned the school last night." It was a tense kind of time in the city.

I was there [the Irving School meeting, September 10th], I remember Berry presented this plan. I am sitting there listening. I thought it sounded feasible. It was quite a meeting. There was a lot of talk about what's going to happen when the kids get sick, they will be so far away. I can remember, it was a kind of emotional meeting.

They were upset because [the school district] was talking about doing something with their kids. I remember Josie Stewart said, "These are our kids you're talking about." She made some good points. They hired her, too. She ended up working for the district, I think she worked as a liaison between the district and the community.

At that time, I was teaching at Emerson. We went to the meetings and we listened, but we didn't think that Emerson was going to be involved. That was in the fall, and then in February, . . . before the [district-wide] busing, this was the first group that they moved [as a part of the integration plan]. They took children from Emerson and sent them to Hyatt and Highland.

In fact we rode the bus as a visitation, so I literally rode the bus with the kids.

And I was selected to go with the children to Highland School. That was a very difficult year for me as a teacher because I had children from two different schools and from about three or four classrooms. So I thought, My gosh, what am I going to do with these kids? Then I thought, "Individualized instruction." We went there right away, because the students were all over the place in their abilities, and where they could be.

There were several incidents, and I think they could have worked with the teachers more. . . . There was one little girl, I guess she was in the fifth grade or sixth grade. The teacher [was counting the students] and said "eenie, meenie, miney, mo" and she said the whole thing.

Well, when I got home I got a call from the mother. She said, "Sue, do you know what this woman said in the classroom?" When I heard, I said, "Oh my." She said, "I will be there tomorrow to talk to the principal." And she was.

I saw her come in. Well the teacher said, "Oh Sue, I don't know why I said it." I said, "I don't know why you did, either." The teachers needed some help.

One little boy, I'll never forget him, Darrell, he was one of my favorite kids. We were grouping these kids, cause we were team teaching and had first, second, and third graders together. He was third grade, and he had

. . . Strickland continued on page 89

possible reverse boycott. Then the naval officer, who had presented the opposition petition to the Board, got control of the meeting. He said, "We saw democracy at work. We had a chance to be heard. You heard the School Board members. They're obviously sincere in what they believe. They deserve a chance to see if the plan works." Basically he persuaded the opposition group to dissolve. One never knows where the people are who are key to a particular situation.

Superintendent Bruce Miller played a relatively minor role in the negotiation of this crisis. Justified or not, he was not trusted by the African-American leaders, so he stepped back and allowed Ray Berry to take the lead for the administration. Miller was a good man. He wrote a statement for the October 18th hearing:

> It is also a time when great changes are taking place. . . . The thing that is disturbing to so many of us is the sudden change. In the present instance, we are experiencing a gigantic civil rights movement which is engulfing the entire nation. Overnight communities all across the country are having to re-think their responsibilities to people. Riverside is not alone in this great social revolution, nor can it hope to turn its head and pretend that change will not take place here. . . . The acceptance of change is one of the great lessons we can capture from the child. It is beautiful to behold how quickly, how completely, children adapt themselves to change. We do not need to fear how the children are to respond to the plan which has been outlined here tonight. . . . During these past days I have sensed, through all the tensions and differences, a unity of purpose and a singleness of goal. . . . The plan which has been presented here tonight is a major step toward that goal. . . . The plan, when it has been carried out, will be an historic occasion for the community. . . . I believe in this proposed plan and would earnestly recommend its adoption.

Implementation of the Plan

In November 1965, the Casa Blanca Study Committee was appointed, consisting of 40 members. It included three members of the Advisory Committee on Integration; three teachers and the principal at Casa Blanca; several other teachers, including Jean Grier, one of the outstanding black teachers in the District whom I knew personally; representatives from the P.T.A. groups at neighboring elementary schools; the principal of Ramona High School; a lawyer; the president of one of the leading banks in town; and representatives of the Casa Blanca community itself. The committee met five times and had finished their work by March 1, 1966, two months ahead of schedule.

The committee was given certain confidential data about the enrollment of Casa Blanca School. The Lorge-Thorndike Nonverbal Test of Ability, designed to measure abstract reasoning ability, showed that Casa Blanca's second grade

Strickland continued from page 87

been in my second grade, and they put him in a first grade math group. I said, "Oh no, no, no, he doesn't belong there, he's good in math."

Well, he stayed one day in first grade math, and the teacher said, "He doesn't belong in that group." I said, "I know." Well, he moved up. He ended up graduating from college as a math major.

I think they needed to be more sensitive to some of the needs of the children. One little boy, they were upset because he was taking other children's lunches. When I looked at his lunch, I thought I would have taken someone else's, too. It was very meager. He was probably hungry.

I think the teachers needed some training probably. Not all of them—some of them were very receptive, and went out of their way to make the children feel comfortable. But I think we could have done more to prepare the teachers for receiving the children. We were getting children from all different classes. I know Esther [Velez Andrews] and Bea [Pavitt] did some work [to prepare students and families]. But [preparing the teachers] was one of the things we could have done a little differently. It was hard, in the middle of the year like that. It was a kind of difficult time.

When you look at the history of Riverside, it was a divided city. And then in the 20s when the Klan came here, it became more so. Early on, blacks lived kind of all over. And then after the 20s, they kind of settled on the Eastside. The Mexicans were not treated so kindly either.

[In Riverside] the jobs were horrible for black people. My mother was born here. My grandparents met and married here. My mother's sisters all left Riverside because there were no jobs. We were offered only menial work. That was all we ever got. Many of the people in Riverside had good educations but they left because they couldn't use them. . . . They all left, because the opportunities were not here.

Then we had this influx of outsiders that were very intelligent and already had jobs. Housing and lots of things changed. Prior, they had had restricted covenants here in housing. [The practice of covenants that restricted the rental, lease, or sale of homes to "whites only" became commonplace starting in the 1920s. In California, a 1959 attempt to legislate fair housing was scuttled by a successful 1964 statewide ballot proposition that allowed property owners to discriminate on the basis of race, religion, or ethnic background. The California Supreme Court struck down the proposition in 1966.]

Things did change. I think the community wanted more at that point. It was a big change. A lot of people came in with degrees, engineers and doctors. The community changed. They were angry. The whole mood of the country was not good, when you look at the killings, and everything that was going on.

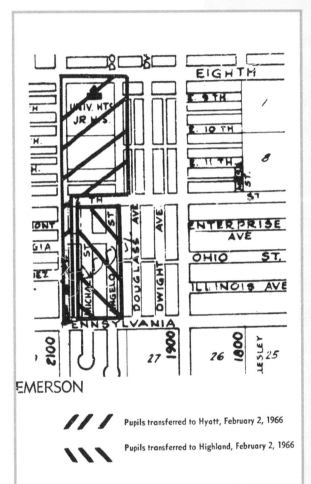

EIGHTH

E. 9TH

E. 10TH

E. 11TH

ST.

ENTERPRISE AVE

OHIO ST.

ILLINOIS AVE

ENNSYLVANIA

EMERSON

/// Pupils transferred to Hyatt, February 2, 1966

\\\ Pupils transferred to Highland, February 2, 1966

Above: Teacher Sue Strickland accompanied students from Emerson to Highland in February 1966. The lessons learned from that integration effort were applied to all other Riverside schools for full integration starting in September 1966. The map above shows how students were transferred (Hendrick, The Development of a School Integration Plan in Riverside, California, A History and Perspective. *248).*

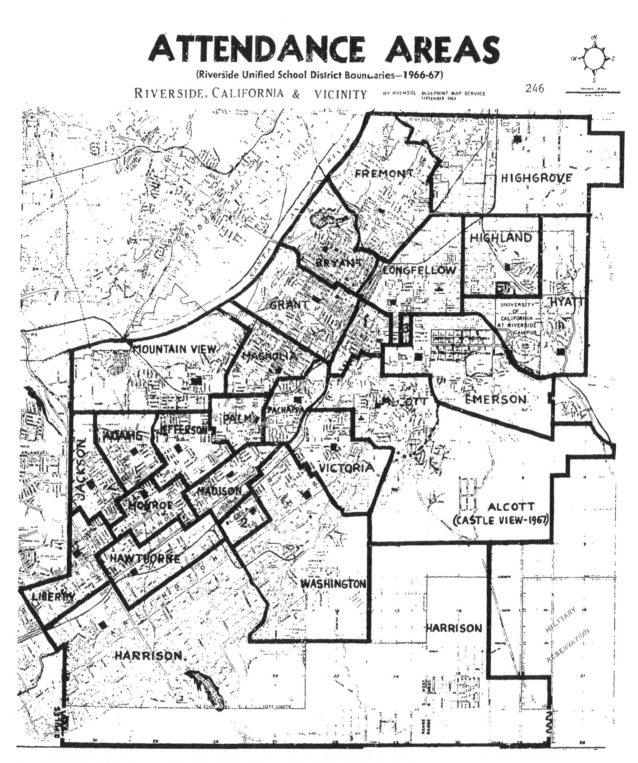

ATTENDANCE AREAS

(Riverside Unified School District Boundaries—1966-67)

RIVERSIDE, CALIFORNIA & VICINITY   BY RIVERSIDE BLUEPRINT MAP SERVICE
SEPTEMBER 1964

246

Above: School attendance area boundaries for 1966–1967. The criteria for assigning students sought to integrate students into classrooms throughout the system. In addition, school planners tried to make sure students from the same families stayed together, that students from the same blocks and small neighborhoods stayed together, and that receiving schools had adequate classroom space. The maps at right show how students were transferred (Hendrick, The Development of a School Integration Plan in Riverside, California, A History and Perspective. *219, 246-248).*

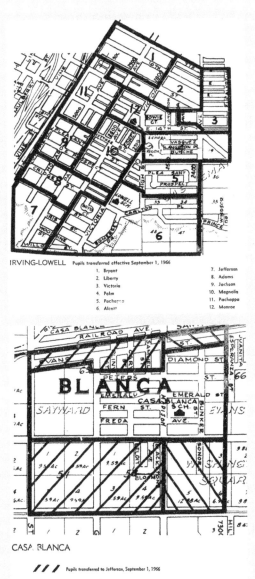

IRVING-LOWELL Pupils transferred effective September 1, 1966

1. Bryant	7. Jefferson
2. Liberty	8. Adams
3. Victoria	9. Jackson
4. Palm	10. Magnolia
5. Pachappa	11. Pachappa
6. Alcott	12. Monroe

CASA BLANCA

/// Pupils transferred to Jefferson, September 1, 1966

\\\ Pupils transferred to Jackson, September 1, 1966

**INTEGRATION OF EMERSON SCHOOL AREA
1966 AND 1968 BOUNDARY CHANGES**

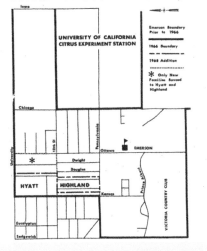

students were ranked last in the district. Other measurement data showed that for all grades, academic achievement in Casa Blanca fell in the lower quartile. The committee members were supplied with information about how segregated education affects achievement. Still, it was going to be a tough job to get community support for the closing of Casa Blanca School and all that it meant.

I can remember speaking at one early meeting during which I was taking questions. One older woman stood up. I am sure that she had not spoken in a public meeting before, and she quietly said, "Mr. Littleworth, I have a son. He went to Casa Blanca, and he's now a barber. Don't you think that is really a good thing? Why do you want to change us?" The thought running through my mind was did your son really want to be a barber, or under different circumstances could he have been a teacher or an engineer or anything else? But to have answered the question in that way would have been rude, so I answered more carefully. "Of course, it was good. And there are lots of good people who have gone through Casa Blanca School. But basically we thought it would be helpful if they began to move into the Riverside community and recognize that in the long run we are all Americans. We are one people and you shouldn't stay isolated in the local Casa Blanca community."

Most of the turn-around in Casa Blanca, however, was due to the work of Ernie Robles. He had gone to school in Casa Blanca and had become a teacher in Riverside and was specially assigned to

Ernest Robles.

this project. He worked tirelessly in meeting after meeting of parents and community leaders to get integration accepted and to close down the Casa Blanca School. He succeeded. Later Robles worked for the U.S. Department of Education and was honored by Riverside City College as Alumnus of the Year in 1997.

The Casa Blanca Study Committee asked the administration to prepare a plan for integration. That plan called for the transportation of 180 Casa Blanca children to other schools in 1966, and the balance of about 250 children to be transported in 1967. Casa Blanca School would be closed in 1967. The Committee unanimously approved the administration's plan in March 1966.

Citywide integration began in September 1965, when about 260 kindergarten and primary grade pupils were moved from Lowell and Irving Schools to ten different schools in the district. That was a crisis decision resulting from the fire, and there was no time for advance planning.

But with Emerson School it was different. Emerson was scheduled to move approximately 100 minority students in February 1966, to Highland and Hyatt Schools. Planning began in the fall of 1965. Berry and Wall met with Emerson School minority parents to explain the significance of the move. In-service education was provided to acquaint the teachers at Emerson, Highland, and Hyatt with some problems related to intergroup education. The Emerson teachers visited the homes of all the children scheduled to be transferred. Visits were arranged to their new schools. The principals of Highland and Hyatt personally received them. Tours of classrooms and other facilities were conducted, each incoming pupil met his new teacher, and the school program was explained. Other meetings were held with P.T.A. representatives and room mothers, and refreshments were served. The welcoming also continued after school began with the local Highland and Hyatt elementary pupils being the hosts and serving the refreshments.

The Emerson move was an outstanding success. The challenge was to carry over that success to 1,000 pupils throughout the district in the fall of 1966.

I am sure that many parents encouraged their children to welcome the newcomers. In 1965–66, my son, Todd, was at Alcott School. Alcott was the center of the protestors' petition against the integration plan. My marching orders to Todd each day were to welcome the pupils from Lowell and to stop any bullying. But as Bruce Miller said

Denise Matthews: *I remember the night that the fire happened; a lot of the neighbors were coming out into the street, talking about the fact that the school had burned. My main memories were just a lot of confusion, "Where was I going to school, who was my teacher going to be, the classmates I had known from school, would we see each other anymore? Would we end up at the same school?"*

As the days went on, the neighborhood people began to refer to the fire as the "firebombing," as opposed to the "fire."

I had watched the Watts riots on TV, and there were people throwing Molotov cocktails into buildings. And when I started hearing the term firebombing, I started thinking in my mind that someone had thrown a Molotov cocktail into the big building. That was the connection that I made. Then I remember talk in the neighborhood, I never heard a suspect named, but I remember my parents having conversations with other parents initially that they thought somebody white did it, and then over time the speculation was that somebody from right there on Carlton Place had done it. What I remember hearing was that the school board hadn't been acting fast enough to integrate the schools, and that this had been done to force the school board's hand.

From my standpoint, I sort of forgot about Lowell; it was like it was missing from the neighborhood. My focus was on the new school, and going there. We lived right down the street from Lowell. We frequently headed that direction, going down Carlton Street. Just looking over there, and the big building was gone. We could see the rows of the other classrooms that were still in the back and the kindergarten building which eventually turned into the church. That's all that was there. It was so different.

In fact, I didn't find out until years later that some of the kids actually returned to Lowell and continued to go to school there. I didn't know that. I thought that everybody had been dispersed to other schools.

I remember the talk about boycotting. I didn't know what that word meant. I was asking my parents, "What does that mean, we're boycotting?" I don't know what explanation they gave me now, but I can distinctly remember asking them what it meant. I know a lot of people were talking about it.

I also remember the Freedom School. I remember thinking I hadn't been in [the Masonic Lodge] in a long time. We had recess right across the street at Lincoln Park, and that rang a bell because in the summertime we would always go swimming at Lincoln Park. So I thought, "We get to have recess in the park." I remember thinking that was cool.

For me, things started to happen so rapidly after the fire. . . . My parents and the Renfros, they had petitioned the school board; courtesy of that we ended up at Pachappa. It was actually a pretty smooth transition into Pachappa. The first day of school, it seems like we got there late. I can remember my teacher stopping whatever he was doing, and saying this is our new student. . . . I don't remember any problems, getting along with the other kids, everybody made friends really quickly.

. . . Matthews continued on page 95

DENISE MATTHEWS

STUDENT AT LOWELL SCHOOL

When Denise Matthews was a child, her family moved from 12th Street to Carlton Place, just north of the arroyo, on the same street as the Renfros and the Blands. The year before Lowell burned, she was in the same class as Wanda [Poole] Scruggs and Craig Goodwin. After Lowell burned, she transferred to Pachappa. The Renfros moved to the San Jose area during the summer of 1966 when Don Renfro was transferred by his employer, IBM. The Pooles later moved to Rubidoux. It seemed that most of her nearby neighborhood friends had scattered by the time she got to Alcott as a part of the implementation of the integration plan.

She lived in Riverside until she graduated from Riverside Polytechnic High School in 1973, when she went to Los Angeles and attended the University of Southern California on academic scholarship. She graduated with her degree in business administration. Since retiring from a successful career with DuPont, she enjoys traveling and freelance writing.

in his remarks on integration, "We do not need to fear how the children are going to respond to the plan which has been outlined here tonight." And he was right.

My involvement in the planning for 1966 was not so "hands on" as it had been during the crisis leading up to the integration plan. My role was a more traditional leadership and policy role as Board president. But my instructions to the administration were clear: detailed planning was imperative for the plan to be assured of success. I likened that to a law case. You can form a great strategy, but you can stumble over a small detail and lose. Enormous preparation was undertaken for the 1966 fall opening.

The same kind of Emerson-Hyatt-Highland actions and relations were spread district-wide into the receiving schools. But some teachers had never related to African Americans and Mexican Americans. Some teachers had little experience in dealing with pupils of low achievement. Some felt insecure about matters of discipline or dealing with minority parents.

Teachers were essential to the process of integration, and we offered them help in many areas: the first general in-service education for teachers occurred in November 1965. At that time the director of intergroup education went to individual schools to discuss integration. In the summer of 1966 the California Department of Education sponsored a joint effort between the District and UCR on integration in the community. In the following year, 1967, the federal government, under a provision of the Civil Rights Act, provided funds for the seminars held in April, May, August, and November. Part of the program was that Ray Berry would attend the closing session of each seminar and would hear, accept, and respond to suggestions by the group.

Other programs were also developed. While teachers still visited the homes of children about to be moved, most of the home visits were transferred to the Home-School Program, a program financed by Title I of the Elementary and Secondary Education Act of 1965. During the winter and spring of 1966, eleven "Community Aides" made more than 1,500 home visits. All of the aides were minorities. None of them was a professional. Formal education was not a requisite of this position. The only criterion was the ability to assist their neighbors and explain the integration plan.

Title I also financed well-equipped reading rooms and specialist reading teachers in eight elementary schools and all junior high and high schools. Not only minorities but also low-income families were eligible for help. Children needing help were transported to the eight centers if their own schools did not have a reading room. All in all, more than 400 children were involved, with each child experiencing forty minutes of individualized instruction four days a week.

Matthews continued from page 93

My parents, the Renfros, and the Pooles, got together to work out the transportation to get us all back and forth to Pachappa. . . . Since my parents both worked at Harris Company, my father would take us to school when he was taking my mother to work.

His afternoon coffee break was right around the time we were getting out of school, and he worked out an arrangement with his boss where he could take an extra 10 or 15 minutes. Most of the time he would pick us up and take us home. He would take everybody back to our house, and everybody was in walking distance from there. Occasionally, the other parents would chip in with some of the driving if he couldn't get away in the afternoons. But I think he was the transportation every morning for us to get to school and most times for us to get home in the afternoon as well.

I don't remember there being any problems until the next year, when I ended up at Alcott for sixth grade.

I am guessing that this may have been the first day or first week of school. I remember a group of white parents at the entrance or near the entrance to the school. They were yelling. I am assuming this was a protest of some sort over the black children coming into Alcott. I can't remember the specifics; I can just remember a group of parents standing at the entrance to the school yelling.

I was not bused to Alcott, either. My parents would take me to school. I don't remember how long that went on. They would take me to school, and they would pick me up. I remember later in the year I started riding my bike to school. I would go down the hill through the golf course, which I thought was the most fun thing in the world, cruising down that hill.

Top: After the Lowell School fire, the upper grades were housed in this remaining building and one other like it until the school was closed in September 1966.

Bottom: The Masonic Hall, one of the Freedom School sites.

My mother was very fair also, and the kids did not recognize that my mother was black. My father was visibly black. I can remember my father picking me up from school one day [and] some of the white kids taking note. . . . And being teased and being taunted about that for quite some time, "Denise has a n_____ father." I can very distinctly remember that. And that went on for quite some period of time. There was one boy who was kind of the ringleader. I can still remember his name to this day.

I can also remember that being a very confusing time. Because in our home, and most of the kids I grew up with, the black kids, we weren't taught about what I would call racism in our homes, and we really weren't that aware of race, per se. It was all this kind of family of Eastsiders, and we had all grown up together. In fact, there was a white family that lived on Pleasant Street, their name was Jordan, and their son Anthony went to Lowell. At one point, Anthony probably wasn't the only white kid, but he was one of the few white kids left at Lowell. And we never thought

. . . Matthews continued on page 97

95

There was an additional reading room established at the now-empty Irving School for more serious reading disabilities. The program was held in six classrooms and was staffed by teachers, a psychologist, a speech therapist, a hearing pathologist, and a nurse.

And there were the successful lessons learned from the Highland and Hyatt School experiences: school visits to the receiving schools, meet your new teacher, teacher aides, UCR tutors, parent volunteers, P.T.A. activists, and welcoming receptions.

Since complex busing was involved, practice runs were scheduled before school began in September 1966. Parent volunteers stood with groups waiting for the bus. And later, we had in-service training for bus drivers about their role in making integration a success.

All in all, we had enormous preparation so that integration was meaningful and was not merely desegregation.

Before the opening of school in September 1966, I again addressed the whole faculty in the auditorium of Ramona High School. The auditorium holds 1,200 people and it was jammed. I outlined the preparations that had been made for a successful integration but I emphasized that continued success depended on the classroom teacher. I spoke to them about what was expected of them. This was a fragile situation in which a single racial incident could blow things sky high. Every teacher became a highly influential person; each one had to solve every problem that arose and do it satisfactorily. There were going to be problems where there was no preparation or direction, and the teacher would have to simply jump in and take care of every one of them. We had to be right all of the time, and we couldn't afford to have bad decisions. The message that day was, "Don't blow it for everybody."

It was a good speech and the teachers were very supportive. The opening day in this historical fall of 1966 went forward without a hitch.

Matthews continued from page 95

of Anthony as the white kid or different; he was just part of the Eastside family. So there wasn't this really strong awareness of a racial divide.

Even though I don't look visibly black, for the most part, growing up in the neighborhood where everybody knew us, there was never any question about who we were or that we were black. Even at Pachappa, that never really came up as an issue. All of a sudden I get to Alcott, and I'm being called all these names that I knew were derogatory. It was confusing for me, because I knew I was black, but I looked like the white kids. And my parents had never really talked to me about that.

Above: Denise Matthews' sixth grade class at Alcott School. Denise is in the top row, second from left.

It was just really confusing because here are these people calling me names, but I look like them, but I knew I wasn't the same as them. That was a really rough year . . .

I remember my sixth grade teacher, Miss Sandusky. I don't remember her treating me any other way than the way she treated the rest of the students. But my parents told me that she would send progress reports home, and the progress reports would always reflect her surprise that I was doing as well in class as the white kids. There was a presumption that either because I was black or because I had come from Lowell, that I wouldn't have been on their level. I had always been a straight A student. I can remember that really bothering my parents and in fact, my parents having some parent–teacher conferences with her to discuss it.

The good thing was that, even though sixth grade was a tough year, it exposed me to different people who had a different way of life from what I had known, [it] forced me into a different world and showed me there was something other than the Eastside. The other side of the golf course was a world that I knew existed, but that we didn't really venture into, because we didn't belong over there.

Moving from 12th Street in Riverside to Carlton Place was a pretty daring thing in 1960. I can remember people from the old neighborhood on 12th Street asking my parents, "Why do you want to go over there. It's just going to be you over there."

I didn't really understand what the big deal was about moving. It was the American dream, "We're moving to a nicer neighborhood now, a neighborhood that's integrated." I didn't really understand what integrated meant at five years old, but I knew we were moving some place that was different from where we had been. But even though we moved to Carlton Place, most of what we did or the people we interacted with were still Eastside. You never really made that leap to the other side of the golf course and what life was like over there, so it was always this kind of mystery. I guess what fifth and sixth grade did for me was show me what that was, and it was within the realm of something I could achieve if I worked hard enough. Had it not been for that, I think I would have grown up in more of a closed world.

It did get better. I remember over time, the name-calling stopped.

MRS. RUTH BRATTEN   ARTHUR LITTLEWORTH   JOHN WENTZ

Top citizens of 1966 announced by the Riverside Civic League

The Press-Enterprise *reported the 1966 annual awards of the Riverside Civic League: Ruth Bratten was named outstanding woman; Arthur Littleworth, outstanding elected official; and John Wentz, outstanding appointed official.*

CHAPTER 7 — EPILOGUE

Scarcely a meeting of the School Board or the administration went by after 1966 without discussion of some phase of the integration program: unused space at Irving and Casa Blanca; the recruitment of more minority teachers; the budget; attention to the racial balance in the junior high schools; reassignment of principals; applications to the federal government to assist in integration; changes in school boundaries; progress in integrating the schools; and a thousand more details.

During the first year of integration, we had an incident that threatened to bring about a renewal of our racial crisis. A black mother, Mrs. Louise George, had a particular complaint which she took to the principal's office of Washington School. The principal was Frank Gibson, who had been vocal in his opposition to the Board's action on integration. We thought about removing him, but he was the symbol to those in Riverside who thought the Board had caved in to pressure resulting from the burning of Lowell School. His removal would have posed another potential crisis. The mother and the principal turned a conversation about her complaint into a shouting match. Then Mrs. George, who was a large woman, reached across the desk and whacked the principal, knocking him down. Gibson called the police and Mrs. George was charged with criminal assault. Well, the School Board couldn't condone anyone hitting a principal or teacher. Still, from the minority point of view, Gibson was a racist and deserved to be hit. Gibson was waiting for the administration and the Board to put pressure on him to dismiss the legal complaint, but we didn't.

Instead, I went to the district attorney personally. I had known Byron Morton since January 1951. We had been sworn to the bar on the same day and celebrated with dinner that evening at the Squire Arms in the Mission Inn, clearly the best restaurant in town at the time.

At this meeting, I said to him, "Byron, you have got to dismiss the complaint. This has a potential for another racial crisis." He replied, "Oh, Art, the complaint was filed. I can't do anything. The law says it must go to trial." Well, that's not true. I knew that the district attorney had wide discretion and I finally got him to agree to at least slow things down. Meanwhile, I tried to calm things down with the community and tried to not lose the support of the teachers and at the same time to not incite another problem with the black community.

As time passed, things began to calm down. I continued to meet with the district attorney, and a month later he dismissed the complaint. So even though we had avoided escalation into a big issue, it was the kind of thing that I was worried about— the kind of incident that could happen and cause the whole community to flare up.

We had an invaluable troubleshooter who worked with the students. Dell Roberts was an African American with a football player's build and a great smile. He was loved by students and parents and was honored by numerous organizations, including the Riverside Unified School District and the city of Riverside. He retired from the District in 2003, after 38 years of service. We had each other's telephone numbers, and he used to call me if there were any threatened racial school fights. There were not many. And I would call him if I heard about any racial disturbance. He was a football coach and he had other duties, but it was great to have a friend on the inside.

There was prompt attention to discipline problems. I can remember one incident at University Junior High School. We got word from parents, about 9:30 p.m., that there was going to be a gang fight the next day. By 11:30 that night we had a plan, and in the morning there were qualified people to handle the problem.

Riverside could be justly proud of its achievement—the first voluntary integration of any large school district in the United States. It had been a harmonious transition, not ordered by the federal court resulting in "white flight." The teachers, administration, and parents were determined to make it work—to create greater educational opportunities for minorities while still preserving the rights of the majority.

The voters of Riverside must have been satisfied with the performance of their School Board members. There was a School Board election in November 1966, with two seats open. The terms were expiring for Mrs. Kendrick and me, and we both filed for reelection. This was an opportunity to substantially change the School Board, but only one challenger, Raymond P. Horspool, filed. He ran on an anti-integration platform and was defeated by a two-to-one majority. *The Press-Enterprise* editorial strongly supported the reelection of Mrs. Kendrick and me:

> Riverside has blessed itself with a first class School Board. And there have been few times in the history of this state when it has been as important to have skilled and sensible policy makers on its local school boards. The present elected representatives of the people of the Riverside Unified School District have guided the schools through a period of considerable crisis with enlightened effectiveness. . . . Arthur Littleworth has, as president, been the guiding spirit of the Board, and an excellent one. Suffice it to say, the community could hope for no better man to head its Board of Education.

A UCR study interviewed parents every year for ten years after the integration. They found support for the integration program for the first year or two in the 90 percent range. This was for all elements of the community—white, African American, and those in Casa Blanca. While the support dropped off a little in later years, the support still remained high.

The Riverside Teacher's Association nominated the Board for a state award, and State Superintendent of Public Instruction Max Rafferty (an outspoken conservative) wrote, "I know of no school board in the United States which has done more on its own initiative to solve the problems of ethnic imbalance in its schools." In May 1966, the National Education Association (NEA) presented an award to the Riverside Unified School District for "distinctive merit" for its efforts in school integration. I was one of three recipients of the Riverside Civic League award as an "Outstanding Citizen" for 1966.

On April 15, 1967 I received a telegram from Governor Ronald Reagan, asking me if I could see him in Sacramento on April 25, 1967. He had just taken office in January of 1967. The telegram read:

> I would like to discuss with you some of the urgent educational problems currently confronting our minority communities. I know that these problems are of great concern to you also, and I am very hopeful, therefore, that you will be able to meet with me on Thursday, April 25 from 9:30 to 11:00 a.m. here in my office in Sacramento. Please notify Mrs. Lee Simonds of our press department whether or not you will be able to attend.
>
> Sincerely, Ronald Reagan.

I accepted. I don't remember who the other people were, but there were four or five of us from school districts around the state. We were ushered into the conference room right next to the governor's office. The door opened, and he came in. He was a very handsome person and, I remember, tall. He was about six-foot-two. He had

WILLIAM O. MEDINA
STUDENT AT LOWELL SCHOOL

William Medina was a first grade student when Lowell burned. His parents, Oscar and Josephine Medina, opened Zacatecas Restaurant in 1963 at the corner of Park and University Avenues. In 1985, it relocated two blocks away, on University Avenue, and remains an important fixture in the Eastside community.

He attended Riverside City College and went on to get a degree and teaching certificate from University of California, Riverside. He alternated periods of teaching high school and working at the restaurant, including caring for his father after a stroke. William Medina earned a PhD in history at UCR. His thesis focused on The Sherman Institute, the residential Indian high school located on Magnolia Avenue in Riverside. His grandmother was a student there. Today he is an adjunct professor of American history at Riverside City College and San Bernardino Valley College.

William Medina: *I disagree that Riverside integrated voluntarily. It wasn't really voluntary, if you look at the circumstances, the context. It was the civil rights movement, Watts is burning in August '65, and then the following month, they burn down the school. All that is adding to the tension in Riverside plus what is going on nationally. In addition, Riverside was in the wrong, legally, so they had to act.*

I remember hearing about the fire, you could smell the smoke. I must have been seven years old. My friends and I walked to the school. Big pile of rubble, and sure enough the fire department closed it off. I remember going home and getting a wagon, and somehow we were able to cross the barricades and pick out books, put the books in the wagon and take them home. I can't recall details, because I was a kid. But I knew there was tension about where we were going to school. I remember going to Freedom School, it was one day. We went to a church, Victoria and 11th, our classroom was in the basement. My dad and Mr. Carlos, Jess Carlos, he owned a grocery, brought boxes of cookies and chips for the kids. We had a blast. I don't remember sitting down, no academics, but I remember running around playing.

We knew we were going to be bused to white schools. All the boys on the block, just little kids, seven years old, we were afraid because we were scared of white people. I don't remember ever talking to a white kid. Then we were going to this white school. We knew a little about prejudice, we heard parents' conversations. So we started teaching ourselves karate. In my dad's front yard, learning self-taught karate, because we were going to defend ourselves, going to this white school. We were worried about being attacked.

I remember going to Pachappa the first time, seeing a kid with blond hair, sitting right behind him. I had never been that close to anyone with blond hair. I was mesmerized by that blond hair, straight, neat. I am sure they had the same reaction. They would stare at us too.

My mom at the restaurant would make us burritos for school. The kids would laugh. I am seven or eight years old, I'm thinking they're laughing at me because I had a tortilla. So I didn't do that again. I took peanut butter and jelly sandwiches. Different times, these white kids didn't know what a tortilla was.

At first it's mutual suspicion, but it breaks down . . . . It didn't last very long, it wasn't very serious. All that eventually evaporated.

My dad was happy with the busing at first, but it was inconvenient, we had to get up early and catch the bus at the school site, but later on they set up bus stops closer to our homes. It did fragment the Eastside because there were kids just a few blocks away I had no contact with, I did not meet them until I went to Central Middle School. The only thing I remember my dad complaining about, is that the busing was one way. "It's not fair, we're being bused to the white schools, why aren't they being bused? Why isn't it both ways?" For me, the busing experience, although inconvenient, was great. Otherwise I would never have had that contact with white kids. I think it helped me out later in life because psychologically, I didn't feel inferior, I felt more confident.

an impressive physical presence with broad shoulders, a trim waist, and a big smile. He came in and said, "I'm Ron Reagan," and he went around the table and shook everybody's hand.

He had no Secretary of Education, no aides, no secretaries of any kind with him, it was him alone. He sat down and told us that he just wanted to talk to us about school matters, and what we'd learned about racial problems. And so for several hours we just talked with him.

Above: Telegram from Governor Reagan.

He gave me ample time and I went through my experiences from 1965–66, stressing the alienation that the minorities felt, and what we might do in making minorities feel a part of the majority community and share in the American dream. I added that those of us in power ought to listen and do what we could to restore faith in government—and to all authority.

What kind of an effect that may have had or didn't have on school matters in California we'll never know, but it was impressive: first his interest in school racial matters; second that he had no administrative staff there.

A short time after the integration plan was approved, *Time Magazine* also contacted the Riverside administration about sending a team to do a national story on the Riverside experience. I didn't want more publicity. I wanted just to be alone for a year or two to get this integration program organized and make it work. And I thought we could do a better job if we were not in the national spotlight. I worried that outside community groups might well use Riverside to foster their own interests. We had had an example of this when out-of-town interests temporarily captured the leadership of the boycott movement. Outside groups could well try to influence the program or the Board election coming up in the fall of 1966. So I directed Mr. Miller to turn down *Time Magazine*. And we never heard from them again.

Later on, in 1972, we did make the national news, and the timing was more appropriate. Tom Wicker, who then was a famous columnist for *The New York Times* and other newspapers and whose column appeared occasionally in *The Press-Enterprise*, came to Riverside as a guest lecturer at UCR. Somehow he found out about our integration efforts and he asked me for an interview. It was a long, relaxed conversation and it turned out to be a laudatory article.

ESTHER [VELEZ] ANDREWS

SUPERVISOR, COMMUNITY AIDE PROGRAM

After Lowell was burned, Ray Berry enlisted Esther [Velez] Andrews' help to facilitate the transition for students in the lower grades and to help develop the integration program. Being bilingual, she was especially valuable in helping to explain the changes to Spanish-speaking parents in the early days of the transfers. Ray Berry named her to supervise the community aides hired to facilitate the integration process. She set up the aide program at Pachappa School, conducted training, and was joined later that year by Beatrice Pavitt. She stayed in the position for a few years, until she returned to teaching at Emerson.

Esther [Velez] Andrews: *I'll tell you a little incident that happened as the busing was going on. Moving these children, kindergarten through grade three, from Lowell, I got a report back from one of the community aides that kids didn't want to get on the bus. They had different places throughout the Eastside where the buses would pick them up at 6:30 in the morning to take these little babies to schools they didn't want to go to.*

I went to the bus stop and asked them what happened. They said, "Oh they're mean to us, they're ugly, they tell us to go home."

I said, "Who?"

They said, "All those women and men at Alcott School."

So I said, "Okay, I am getting on the bus with you." So I got on the bus with them. The bus goes to Alcott; it pulls into that circle in front of the school.

The students said, "You see, Miss Velez. There they are, there they are."

It was all parents lined up along Alcott School. I thought, "What? Parents?"

I said, "Okay, here's the plan, you get off and I'll be the last one to get off."

Sure enough, they get off, and the parents start jeering at them. "Go home. What are you doing here? This is our school."

I am standing at the edge of the bus, hearing them. I let all the students get off and then I get off. I walked over to them. They looked at me, and they were shocked. They did not expect it. I had my badge. I said, "My name is Esther Velez, I am a representative of this district. I am ashamed. I am appalled at what you are doing as parents." They turned their backs and started walking away. I kept talking to them, chastising them. "This is unheard of. You should care about kids, no matter what kids they are."

Then I walked into the principal's office. He was sitting in his office. I walked in, and I said, "Do you realize what's happening out there? In fact, I know you realize what's happening out there. Why haven't you done anything? Allowing those parents, before those kids can start school, to yell at them."

He looked at me and said, "There's nothing I can do about it."

I walked out of there and I went to Ray Berry and I told him what was happening. He was angry. I said, "Fire him, fire him. He's incompetent."

The best school was Jackson. The principal did his homework. He took students, fifth and sixth graders, and made them ambassadors. He told them what their job was. He told them that these kids were coming to their school, they were new and they were afraid, and that they were to befriend them. He did a marvelous job. Those kids met a new kid on the bus; each one had a partner. As each one got off, they escorted them, they spent the day with them. The kids were saying, at the end of the day, "Mr. Nelson, they need to come back, they're our friends. They're wonderful, they have to come back." He just embraced it, the teachers embraced it. They did a marvelous job with it. He was quite a principal.

His column, which appeared in *The New York Times* on March 2, 1972, was titled "No Easy Way." It began with a quote from me, "To improve the education of kids is a lot harder than we thought it would be."

This is even more true under our present circumstances with the United States dropping far behind Asia and Europe in effective education. However, in that interview I was referring to integration from our experience. The community doesn't get educational improvement merely because one black pupil is sitting next to a white pupil.

Desegregation is different from true integration. In 1970, Pasadena was the first non-Southern city ordered by the federal court to desegregate its public school system. The remedy was forced busing, including white children to black schools, resulting in a decade-long bitter battle within the schools.

Boston, however, was the most publicized take-over by the federal courts. In 1974, Judge W. Arthur Garrity, Jr., assumed control of the Boston schools, which lasted until 1988 when the final court case was decided. Between those years there were anti-busing mass movements, boycotts, and protests turning violent with injuries, even deaths. A white teenager was stabbed nearly to death by a black teenager. The community's white residents mobbed the school, trapping the black students inside. After the stabbing, South Boston High was guarded by 500 police officers. In one plan, the court decided that the entire junior class from a mostly white South Boston High School would be bused to Roxbury High School, a black school in a black neighborhood. Half the sophomores from each school would attend the other school, and the seniors could decide what school to attend. For three years Massachusetts State Troopers were stationed at South Boston High School. By the end of the period in 1988, the Boston schools had been reduced from 100,000 students to 57,000, only 15 percent of whom were white.

Riverside's integration program took an enormous amount of detailed planning, and its success in part rested on the adoption of individual personalized instruction. This was a part of Ray Berry's "decentralized" policy—putting the real decisions at the school level, with good people counted on to make good decisions. Education, generally, is more difficult than people realize. Teachers can't do it alone. They need parental help and all the resources a community can provide.

As I said to Tom Wicker, education is but one facet of integration, "I think the need to bring us together as one people is equal to the need for improved education." And today I think that the need to bring us together as one people is even more important.

In May 27, 1997, Dan Bernstein, a columnist with *The Press-Enterprise*, quoted me (quite accurately): "What we need almost more than anything is to remain as one

Craig Goodwin: *I remember it like it was yesterday, because it had a huge impact on those of us going [to the upper grades]. It was a particularly moving experience, because the way Lowell School was set up, you had the ability to move to the big building when you were in fifth grade. The big building housed the principal's office, the nurse's office. You had the ability to be a "safety," meaning that during recesses or before and after school, you actually wore a badge on your arm and you got to be in charge. You would escort the kids that didn't know where they were supposed to be and make sure they were following you to the class. So from kindergarten all the way through fourth grade, you were looking up at the prospect that you're going to be in the big building. And the summer before my fifth grade, the school burned, the big building burned.*

It was devastating. I still remember the smell, the burned books, everything water-logged because we were just a block away. I remember the next day, seeing it burned. It was just a hole in my chest.

It was one of those kinds of life-changing events, actually. And it went from being a life-changing event in a negative way, to going to a new school and meeting a bunch of people who had opportunity, who you actually looked at, and they had things available to them that you had no idea were available.

So [when the district closed Lowell in 1966 and integrated], the one block distance that I traveled to go to school each day [was transformed]. We were this little rag tag group of blacks and browns that were friends, and we crossed the bridge together into this unknown territory, uncharted waters. Our course was either over the Victoria Bridge, or under the Victoria Bridge and through the Victoria County Club, then up the other side and around the curve to Alcott. We rode bikes sometimes, but for the most part we walked. And of course, being 11-year-olds, when we did go under the bridge, [it was great]. There was still a creek running there with tadpoles and crawdads . . . a little stream that went all the way down to the freeway and all the way to RCC [Riverside City College].

So some days we would either take golf balls off the driving range and throw them around on the golf course or hunt down tadpoles. This is at like seven o'clock in the morning, so that by the time you got to school you were probably even dirtier than you were when you were wearing your old clothes. As I think back about it, we were probably quite a sight.

The lifesaving change for me was going to Alcott. I had a black, male teacher in sixth grade and his name was Richard Keppler. That gave me a connection, and he took me under his wing, and there were two significant things that happened to me immediately upon arriving in the classroom. The first day that we were in class, he was introducing himself and asking the kids in the class different questions and he asked, "How many of your parents are doctors and lawyers?"

And I just remember that I laughed out loud, thinking that he was making a joke, because being from Lowell School—although I found later that there were probably two or three children of doctors at Lowell—it wasn't reality

CRAIG GOODWIN
STUDENT AT LOWELL SCHOOL

Craig was a student in Doris [Doskocil] Haddy's class with Denise Matthews and Wanda [Poole] Scruggs when Lowell was burned. Esther [Velez] Andrews was his kindergarten teacher.

He transferred to Alcott when Lowell closed in 1966. Later at Riverside Polytechnic High School, he was president of the Black Students Union and youth president of the NAACP. In 1973, he was a one of the organizers of a United Black Students Union, which included six high schools. He attended San Jose State University and then University of California, Riverside until he left to pursue a successful business career.

. . . Goodwin continued on page 107

people. Segregated schools lead to segregated attitudes, and, I think, take us in the wrong direction."

Superintendent Bruce Miller retired in June 1968, after 38 years as a school administrator. His career had seen explosive growth in the schools, profound changes in school financing, ever-changing ideas about curricula, and a social revolution with respect to race and schools. But I am sure the last two or three years were the most rewarding in his distinguished career.

The usual method of selecting a new superintendent of schools is to hire a search firm, take applications from California and perhaps nationwide, designate a committee to weed out all but the top applications, and present the top applicants, perhaps three or five, for the decision of the Board.

Rather than going through this process, I invited the Board to my home for dessert and coffee. The first issue was whether to hire a search firm and take applications, but it soon became apparent that there was no need for outside help. We had the associate superintendent at hand, and he was the best leader we were apt to find anywhere in the country. The meeting lasted about ten minutes—Ray Berry was unanimously elected the new superintendent of schools. The confidence in him by the Board was borne out by his illustrious career as superintendent. He served until his retirement in 1978, well-loved by all elements in the community.

One of the more compelling arguments against integration had been that the Board's hasty decision was the result of minority pressure and that more time had been needed to study the issue. Of course, the opposition did not understand the background of the decision. They did not know that in 1961 a majority of the Board had been in favor of closing Lowell School. They did not know that in 1963 the Board had considered integration, but with the strong support of the minority community, they had decided instead to make their neighborhood schools better. They did not appreciate the momentum that had picked up in the 1960s to eliminate all kinds of segregation: sit-ins at lunch counters, movies, and hotels; and Freedom Riders to eliminate discrimination on interstate buses and depots.

I had concluded in the first days after the fire that the crisis would get worse if nothing were done, and if we were going to do anything constructive we had better do it at once. To "study" the situation would have been a disaster. To minority groups, the word study is a euphemism for not doing anything. Delay was not going to teach us anything new. So we did what the Board thought was right. Within two days after the fire, we decided that Lowell School would not be rebuilt or go into double sessions but rather that the displaced children would be distributed to other schools with low minority enrollment. Within a week we decided that all three segregated schools, Irving, Lowell, and Casa Blanca, should be integrated and requested thirty

Goodwin continued from page 105

for me. So I laughed out loud. And then two-thirds of the classroom raised their hands to say that they were, in fact, the children of doctors and lawyers or people of significant education.

It checked me into the reality that these things were possible. This is different. I am somewhere else.

The second thing he did is that he added a word to our vocabulary each day. Each day, we had to take a word from the dictionary and work it into a sentence the next day and be able to stand and speak that sentence in front of the class. It made me appreciate words. He put on my report card to my mother that I was intelligent yet loquacious. We raced to the dictionary to figure out if that was a good thing or a bad thing.

It actually helped because I forged some relationships that I still have today from the new kids I met. Ultimately the majority of them went to Gage Junior High School, I went to Central, and then we all came together again at Poly High School, where I went with Todd Littleworth, I think that's Art's son. In fact, I think I beat him in the sophomore class elections for vice president. That was a long, long time ago.

When you talk about my experience having doctors' and lawyers' children in a classroom [as a] majority, not just a rare child here or there, where it was normal, day-to-day, to have that level of achievement, it meant that not only did you graduate from high school but you were expected to go to college. And you were expected to graduate from college and maybe seek some higher degree. So it became a part of your frame of reference, a part of everything that you did every day. You can artificially insert information into a segregated school about what is possible on the other side, but until you are enmeshed in it, until you are a part of it, it's not going to be real.

I think that Riverside had a good approach. Obviously, it couldn't be color-blind, it had to consider [all factors] to make the schools integrated and make the numbers right so that the blacks and the Hispanics and everybody else could be assimilated. But it seemed that there was always some sort of "beyond just the numbers" approach. I don't know if it [originated] all the way back with John North coming here as an abolitionist and a religious figure or that Arthur Littleworth and the people of the time were good people. But it seemed like there was always something that made Riverside care more for people ... because the significance of integration is that it happened without much blueprint around the country of how to do it. We were on the cutting edge. I think the pro-activeness of it had a lot to do with there not being any violence.

There were protests and there was a Freedom School and there were outspoken critics of the status quo, but I think that it was really, really well done, and when I think about it, I think it affected me in a way that was very, very positive in the end. I attribute a lot of my professional success to going through those kinds of things and being able to articulate my concerns and being able to talk to people without having any kind of inferiority complex. Whereas, I think if I had stayed in a segregated school. . . . I still think there would have been a little apprehension about what I was going towards. . . . For me, it just broadened my perspective on what was possible.

days to decide how to do that. And within approximately thirty days, we had a plan for complete integration—a pragmatic plan without developing a deep split in the Riverside community and thereby avoiding a violent confrontation.

I had never realized how left out the minority community felt. They didn't believe anything we said. We had to show people that they could have faith and trust in the leaders of the community. So we just listened, and then we tried to do what we could about the righteous complaints. To the parents, this was an education problem, but it really was a Riverside community problem—the problem of trying to be one people, one community. For a generation or two, we had some success, but times do change.

I shepherded the integration program on its way until my retirement from the Board in 1972. Integration, not desegregation, was secure in the hands of the School Board and Ray Berry at that time.

Those years on the School Board, and particularly my role in the voluntary integration of Riverside's schools, were the most gratifying experience in all my public service years. I have served on the State Educational, Innovation and Planning Commission, 1972–75; as president of Riverside Press Council, 1973–75; as the first president of the Mission Inn Foundation, 1976–78, a non-profit corporation charged with the responsibility of restoring and operating the Mission Inn until its sale by the city; as a member of the Governor's Commission to Review Water Rights Laws, 1977–78; as president of Southern California Water Conference, 1983–85; chairman of the Arlington Heights Greenbelt Study, 1989; as a member of the Mayor's Use of Force Review Panel, 1999; and as a member of the Mayor's Santa Ana River Task Force, 2004. But the most important for me was serving on the Board of Education during the integration process. I hope that race relations were truly improved by my actions.

However, Riverside is changing. Today we have a population of about 300,000, and the city is much more diverse than it was during the sixties. Things are not the same as when Riverside dealt with integration in our schools. But whatever Riverside faces in the future, problems in education or otherwise, let us remind ourselves of the history of the sixties—we are at our best when we are united as one people.

ACKNOWLEDGMENTS

The central events of the integration of schools in Riverside, California, will forever stay with me, but after all these years the details are apt to be suspect. Fortunately, I have been aided in the setting down of this story by meetings and interviews that were taped.

In January 1966, Mr. Bruce Miller and I made a lengthy presentation to the State Board of Education in which I detailed the background leading up to the integration plan, and Mr. Miller and his associate, Dr. Donald Taylor, went over the plan itself.

The State Board asked many probing questions related to the policies of the state as a whole. I emphasized that we talked to the "leaders" of the minority community for a number of years about the problems of education, and we tried to do something to meet their concerns. "I found when we really got down to it, they had not truly opened up to us. This basically has to come out of a lack of trust, and there just wasn't any trust. You have to have some understanding, and get down deeply into the problem." The essential element of integration was building that trust. The dialogue was taped, and I used parts of it in this memoir.

In the spring of 1966, I granted a series of interviews to a graduate student at the University of California, Riverside. The crisis of the previous fall of 1965 was still fresh in my mind, and some of the interviews were recorded and transcribed.

In 1988, I was interviewed by an educational writer, Dorothy F. Wissler, PhD. The meetings were taped and transcribed. It was the first time I had talked about not only the crisis of 1965 but also the implementation of integration from 1966 and beyond. She urged me to write a book letting the general public know that things can be changed, that making these changes proved to be one of the most satisfying aspects of my career. Her research revealed that Riverside became the first large city in the nation to voluntarily develop, without court action, a full-scale integration plan for its schools.

In 2005, the University of California, Berkeley, published my oral history "Water Law Attorney and Riverside Civic Leader." It dealt primarily with my experiences with the law, but there was one part about the integration program in Riverside.

I am deeply indebted to Irving G. Hendrick, history professor at UCR, for *The Development of a School Integration Plan in Riverside, California: A History and Perspective* (1968). I used it for the history of Riverside and its schools when I was not on the School Board (prior to 1958). And I used it to obtain certain statistical information, the names of the citizens' committees, the text of the petition for integration, and some additional reports and statements. It was invaluable since I did not have to go through the school records. It had already been done for me.

I obtained the legal civil rights background in Chapter 3 from copies of the original rulings of the courts. These were provided by the Best Best & Krieger law library. Additional sources include the U.S. Department of State's *Free At Last, The U.S. Civil Rights Movement* and information on the 16th Street Baptist Church bombing and Rosa Parks from Wikipedia.

My good friend, Barbara Shackelton, edited the manuscript for punctuation and grammar rules and gave me valuable recommendations on organization.

Lastly, and most importantly, I want to express my deep gratitude to my wife, Peggy. I wrote this work by hand, and she typed it—with many drafts. Since my stroke, writing is a struggle, tiresome, with the result that my writing style was rather sparse. She gave me encouragement when needed, she filled in words when I knew what I wanted to write but couldn't find the words, and she was a constructive critic. Without her help, these reflections would still be in my mind.

BIBLIOGRAPHY

Books

Berry, Ray, with Dorothy Wissler and Flora Ida Ortiz. *Superintending: A Look at the How of Decentralizing, Restructuring and Reforming Public Schools.* Riverside: School of Education, University of California, Riverside, 1990.

Hendrick, Irving G., *The Development of a School Integration Plan in Riverside, California, A History and Perspective.* Riverside: The Riverside School Study, A Joint Project of the Riverside Unified School District and the University of California, Riverside, State McAteer Project Number M7-14, September 1968.

Patterson, Tom. *A Colony for California.* Riverside: The Museum Press of the Riverside Museum Associates, 1996.

Court Cases

Bell v. School City of Gary, 324 Fed. 209. United States Court of Appeals, Seventh Circuit, 1963.

Browder v. Gayle, 142F. Supp. 707. District Court of the United States for the Middle District of Alabama, Northern Division, 1956.

Brown v. Board of Education of Topeka, 347 U.S. 483. Supreme Court of the United States, 1954.

Brown v. Board of Education, 349 U.S. 294. Supreme Court of the United States, 1955.

Deal v. Cincinnati Board of Education, 369 F. 2d 55, United States Court of Appeals, Sixth Circuit, 1966.

Downs v. Board of Education of Kansas City, 336 F. 2d 988. United States Court of Appeals, Tenth Circuit, 1964.

Hummel v. Allen, 245 N.Y.S. 2d 876. New York, 1963.

Jackson v. Pasadena City School District, 59 Cal. 2d 876. Supreme Court of California, 1963.

Milliken v. Bradley, 418 U.S. 717, Supreme Court of the United States, 1974.

Plessy v. Ferguson, 163 U.S. 537. Supreme Court of the United States, 1896.

Taylor v. Board of Education of New Rochelle, 191 F. Supp. 181. United States Court of Appeals, Second District, 1961.

Swann v. Charlotte-Mecklenburg Board of Education, 402 U.S. 1. Supreme Court of the United States, 1971.

Articles

"16th Street Baptist Church Bombing." *Wikipedia.* Wikimedia Foundation. Web. April 2014.

Bruner, Borgna and Elissa Haney. "Civil Rights Movement Timeline." *Information Please Database,* 2007. Web. April 2014.

"City Upon a Hill." *Wikipedia.* Wikimedia Foundation. Web. April 2014.

"Congress of Racial Equality." *Wikipedia.* Wikimedia Foundation. Web. April 2014.

"Bloody Sunday." *Encyclopedia of Alabama, Alabama Humanities Foundation,* October 2012. Web. April 2014.

"Freedom Riders." *Wikipedia.* Wikimedia Foundation. Web. March 2014.

"Greensboro Sit-ins." *Wikipedia.* Wikimedia Foundation. Web. May 2014.

LaBerge, Germaine and Ruth Langridge. "Arthur L. Littleworth: Water Law Attorney and Riverside Civic Leader." Regional Oral History Office, Bancroft Library of the University of California, Berkeley. Regents of the University of California. 2005. Web. March 2014.

Noel, Ann M. and Phyllis W. Chang. "Through Struggle to the Stars: A History of California's Fair Housing Law." *California Real Property Journal,* Volume 27, Number 4. 2009. Web. April 2014.

"Rosa Parks." *Wikipedia.* Wikimedia Foundation. Web. April 2014.

"Watts Riots." *Wikipedia.* Wikimedia Foundation. Web. April 2014.

Newspapers

Foreman, T.E. "Civil Rights Leaders Deplore School Arson." *The Press*, Press-Enterprise Company (Riverside, CA). C1. September 8, 1965. n.p. Print.

—————— "Lowell, Irving Schools: System, Not Teaching, Blamed for Low Scoring." *Daily Enterprise*, Press-Enterprise Company (Riverside, CA). September 1965. n.p. Print.

—————— "Schools to Study Segregation Issue." *Daily Enterprise*, Press-Enterprise Company (Riverside, CA). July 15, 1965. n.p. Print.

Gordon, Mike. "School—and Symbol—Burned 10 Years Ago Today." *The Press-Enterprise*, Press-Enterprise Company (Riverside, CA). September 7, 1975. n.p. Print.

Graze, Gregory. "Week That Riverside Made Commitment to Desegregate." *The Press-Enterprise*, Press-Enterprise Company (Riverside, CA). January 13, 1963. n.p. Print.

Holmes, Bob. "In No Time, It Was as if They Were Friends, Not Strangers." *Daily Enterprise*, Press-Enterprise Company (Riverside, CA). June 29, 1966. n.p. Print.

Montgomery, John. "Most Pupils Like Freedom School." *The Press*, Press-Enterprise Company (Riverside, CA). September 14, 1965. n.p. Print.

Patterson, Tom. "Arson Guts Lowell School Wing: Segregation Protest Due at Board Meet." *The Press*, Press-Enterprise Company (Riverside, CA). September 7, 1965. n.p. Print.

—————— "Board Sets Double Sessions at Lowell Temporarily." *The Press*, Press-Enterprise Company (Riverside, CA). C1. September 8, 1965. n.p. Print.

—————— "Desegregation Gets Go Ahead." *Daily Enterprise*, Press-Enterprise Company (Riverside, CA). October 26, 1965. n.p. Print.

—————— "Integration Plan to Stress Individual." *The Press-Enterprise*, Press-Enterprise Company (Riverside, CA). October 17, 1965. n.p. Print.

—————— "Riverside School Board, NAACP Discuss Virtually Segregated Schools." *The Press-Enterprise*, Press-Enterprise Company (Riverside, CA). September 1963. n.p. Print.

—————— "School Board Studies Plan to Cut Race Segregation." *The Press*, Press-Enterprise Company (Riverside, CA). November 1, 1963. n.p. Print.

—————— "Schools Official Claims Negro Transfers Okayed." *The Press*, Press-Enterprise Company (Riverside, CA). September 14, 1965. n.p. Print.

"Racial Balance in Schools Shifts Slightly." *The Press*, Press-Enterprise Company (Riverside, CA). October 18, 1965. n.p. Print.

Short, Lee. "Few Leads in Burning of School." *The Press*, Press-Enterprise Company (Riverside, CA). C1. September 8, 1965. n.p. Print.

The Learning Network, "March 7, 1965: Civil Rights Marchers Attacked in Selma Alabama." *New York Times*. March 7, 2012. Web. March 2014.

"Top Citizens of 1966 announced by the Riverside Civic League." *The Press*, Press-Enterprise Company (Riverside, CA). 1966. n.p. Print.

Wicker, Tom. "No Easy Way." *New York Times*. March 2, 1972. n.p. Print.

Government Publications

California Education Code.

California Department of Education. *California Laws and Policies Relating to Equal Opportunities in Education.* Sacramento, CA. 1964. 18 pp.

California Governor's Commission on the Los Angeles Riots, John A. McCone, Chairman. *Violence in the City: An End or a Beginning?* The Commission. Los Angeles, CA. December 2, 1965. Web. May 2014.

Freidman, Michael Jay and George Clack and Mildred Sola Neely; Eds. *Free At Last, The U.S. Civil Rights Movement.* U.S. Department of State, Bureau of International Information Programs. Washington, DC. December 29, 2008. 72 pp.

U.S. Census Bureau. Census of Population: 1950, *Characteristics of the Population.* Vol. II, part 5, California. Washington, D.C. U.S. Government Printing Office. 1952. 483 pp.

——————U.S. Census of Population and Housing: 1960, *San Bernardino, Riverside, and Ontario, California.* PHC (1)-135. Washington, D.C. U.S. Government Printing Office. 1961.

U.S. Navy. "NSWC Corona Division, Command History." Commander Naval Sea Systems Command, Washington Navy Yard, DC. Web. March 2014.

Other Sources

"Black Enlisted Men's Club" 1942. Captured from *Camp Anza, World War II Army Staging Camp In Riverside.* Video. 2011. *YouTube.* Web. May 2014.

"John Sotelo" Captured from *Down By The Riverside.* City of Riverside. Video. 2008. *YouTube.* Web. May 2014.

Path to Understanding, 1989. Riverside Unified School District, 1989. Video.

"The Ku Klux Klan in the 1920s." *Fatal Flood. American Experience.* PBS. WGBH Educational Foundation, Boston. 2001. Television.

Unpublished Documents

Berry, Ray. "Supplemental Report on Instruction." Riverside, CA: Riverside Unified School District, May 17, 1965.

Riverside Unified School District. "Minutes of the Board of Education of Riverside Unified School District, June 19, 1961" (Lowell Study Committee Report). Riverside, CA: Riverside Unified School District.

——————"Minutes of the Board of Education of Riverside Unified School District, March 18, 1963" (Direction to start to include ethnic composition in school boundary decisions). Riverside, CA: Riverside Unified School District.

——————"Minutes of the Board of Education of Riverside Unified School District, October 7, 1963" (Proposals by Ray Berry re: *de facto* segregation). Riverside, CA: Riverside Unified School District.

——————"Minutes of the Board of Education of Riverside Unified School District, September 21, 1964" (Compensatory Education progress). Riverside, CA: Riverside Unified School District.

——————"Minutes of the Board of Education of Riverside Unified School District, October 5, 1964" (Extend Lowell, Irving, and Casa Blanca transfer policy to all grades). Riverside, CA: Riverside Unified School District.

——————"Minutes of the Board of Education of Riverside Unified School District, May 17, 1965" (Ray Berry's Supplemental Report on Instruction including Compensatory Education). Riverside, CA: Riverside Unified School District.

——————"Minutes of the Board of Education of Riverside Unified School District, September 7, 1965" (Petition to desegregate, Lowell School fire). Riverside, CA: Riverside Unified School District.

——————"Minutes of the Board of Education of Riverside Unified School District, September 13, 1965" (Special meeting to consider petition to desegregate). Riverside, CA: Riverside Unified School District.

————— "Minutes of the Board of Education of Riverside Unified School District, September 20, 1965" (Advisory committee formed for desegregation plan). Riverside, CA: Riverside Unified School District.

————— "Minutes of the Board of Education of Riverside Unified School District, October 4, 1965" (Advisory committee members). Riverside, CA: Riverside Unified School District.

————— "Minutes of the Board of Education of Riverside Unified School District, October 18, 1965" (Presentation of Proposed Master Plan for Desegregation). Riverside, CA: Riverside Unified School District.

————— "Minutes of the Board of Education of Riverside Unified School District, October 25, 1965" (Approval, Proposed Master Plan for Desegregation). Riverside, CA: Riverside Unified School District.

————— *Riverside Unified School District History and Plot Plans.* Mimeo. Riverside, CA. November 1964.

Riverside Unified School District Office of the Superintendent. Program and Curriculum [for Compensatory Education]. Riverside, CA: Riverside Unified School District. September 16, 1963.

—————Proposed Master Plan for School Integration. Riverside, CA: Riverside Unified School District. October 18, 1965.

Sharp, B. Rae. "School Board Memo Report on Conference Re: Segregated Schools, September 16, 1963, Monday" Riverside, CA: Riverside Unified School District Board Memo. September 16, 1963.

Photographs

Alice Key Portrait. n.d. Web. February 2014. riversider.org.

Ben Lewis Portrait. n.d. City of Riverside.

Cockerell, Sue. *Ted Neff. Davis Enterprise.* November 12, 2013. Web. April 2014.

Ernest Robles Portrait. n.d. *Hispanic Scholarship Fund.* Web. April 2014.

Etienne Caroline Portrait. n.d. Web. February 2014. riversider.org.

Gay Caroline Portrait. n.d. Web. February 2014. riversider.org.

Haddy, Doris. *Wing of Lowell School.* n.d.

Irving School 1891—1955. n.d.

Iwasaki, Carl. *The Plaintiffs In Brown v. Board of Education. Topeka, Kansas,* 1953. Time Life Pictures/Getty Images.

Lowell School. n.d.

Lowell School Reunion. 2009.

McCulloh, Douglas. *John Gabbert, Dell Roberts, Sue Strickland, Jesse Wall.* 2013. *Esther Velez Andrews, Robert Bland, Tyree Ellison, Charles Field, Craig Goodwin, Doris Doskocil Haddy and Barbara Wheelock Hamilton, Irving School Auditorium, Masonic Hall, Denise Matthews, William Medina, Walter Parks, Wanda Poole Scruggs, Ruth Bratten Anderson Wilson, Dorothy Wissler.* 2014. Used by permission.

Max Rafferty Portrait. n.d. Web. April 2014.

Mission Inn—Riverside, Calif. n.d. Vintage postcard. Collection of Steve Lech. April 2014.

National Guard Education Foundation. *Soldiers of California's 40th Armored Division Direct Traffic Away from an Area of South Central Los Angeles Burning During the Watts Riots.* 1965. *Wikipedia.* Wikimedia Commons. Web. February 2014.

New York World Telegram. *Burning Buildings During Watts Riots.* August 1965. *Wikipedia.* Wikimedia Commons. Web. February 2014.

Photograph of Mrs. Rosa Parks with Dr. Martin Luther King, Jr. (ca. 1955). National Archives and Records Administration Records of the U.S. Information Agency Record Group 306, 1955. *Wikipedia.* Wikimedia Commons. Web. February 2014.

Parks, Walter. *Bruce Miller, Art Littleworth, B. Rae Sharp.* n.d.

_____ *Casa Blanca School.* n.d.

_____ *Grant School.* n.d.

_____ *Irving School.* n.d.

_____ *Ray Berry.* n.d.

Ringquist, Bob. *Lowell Arson Investigation. The Press,* September 7, 1965.

Robert Bland Portrait. n.d. *University of Virginia.* Web. February 2014.

United Press International. *Freedom Riders Arrive in Anniston, Alabama, May 14, 1961.* National Museum of American History. Web. April 2014.

U.S. Army. *Operation Arkansas: A Different Kind of Deployment. Soldiers from the 101st Airborne Division escort the Little Rock Nine students into the all-white Central High School in Little Rock, Arkansas, 1957.* National Archives. *Wikipedia.* Wikimedia Commons. Web. February 2014.

U.S. Department of Justice. *Bloody Sunday. Wikipedia.* Wikimedia Commons. Web. February 2014.

New York World Telegram & Sun. *Sit in protestors Ronald Martin, Robert Patterson, and Mark Martin at the F. W. Woolworth luncheon counter in Greensboro in 1960.* Library of Congress. Web. February 2014.

Wesselman, Cliff. *Search for Weapons, Watts Riots.* 1965. Herald Examiner Collection, Los Angeles Public Library, 1966. *Wikipedia.* Wikimedia Commons. Web. February 2014.

Wilson Riles Portrait. n.d. *JoinCalifornia: Election History for the State of California.* Web. April 2014.

Interviews

Andrews, Esther [Velez]. Personal Interview. October 28, 2013.

Anderson Wilson, Ruth [Bratten]. Personal Interview. October 28, 2013.

Bland, Robert. Personal Interview. January 16, 2014.

Ellison, Tyree. Personal Interview. June 1, 2014.

Field, Charles. Personal Interview. May 11, 2014.

Gabbert, John. Personal Interview. July 2, 2013.

Goodwin, Craig. Personal Interview. March 6, 2014.

Haddy, Doris [Doskocil]. Personal Interviews. January 5 and January 9, 2014.

Hamilton, Barbara [Wheelock]. Personal Interviews. January 5 and January 9, 2014.

Matthews, Denise. Personal Interview. January 14, 2014.

Medina, William. Personal Interview. May 15, 2014.

Parks, Walter. Personal Interview. October 24, 2013.

Roberts, Dell. Personal Interview. July 14, 2013.

Scruggs, Wanda [Poole]. Personal Interview. February 26, 2014.

Strickland, Sue. Personal Interview. October 27, 2013.

Wall, Jesse. Personal Interview. January 8, 2014.

Wissler, Dorothy. Personal Interviews. March 11 and 18, 2014.

INDEX

ABOUT THE AUTHOR
ARTHUR L. LITTLEWORTH

The honors and recognitions conferred on Arthur L. Littleworth are numerous, but at the top of the list is his appointment as a "Special Master" by the United States Supreme Court in a precedent setting water rights case between the States of Kansas and Colorado involving the Arkansas River. Despite this honor, however, Arthur is most proud of his service as a member of the Riverside Unified School District Board of Education from 1958 to 1973, and as President from 1962 to 1973. In this role, he was responsible for leading the district in the voluntary integration of the Riverside School system, the first school district with more than 20,000 students to do so in the nation.

Born and raised in Los Angeles, Arthur went to Yale University on a full scholarship earning a Bachelor of Arts with Honors in American History. He later entered the U.S. Navy and saw battle in the Pacific during the final months of World War II. Returning home he proceeded to earn a Master of Arts in American History from Stanford University and law degree from Yale Law School in 1950. That same year he joined Best Best & Krieger, today one of California's major law firms with more than 200 attorneys in 9 offices. He went on to become senior partner, where he led the water law practice group. He was named as one of the "Top 100" lawyers in California, 2001 and 2003, by the Daily Journal, California's legal newspaper, and was listed in "The Best Lawyers in America" for Natural Resources Law. He is the co-author of California Water (1995) and California Water II (2008). His professional recognitions include "The Erwin Chemerinsky Defender of the Constitution Award" from the Federal Bar Association, "Premier Water Attorney" from the Water Education Foundation, "Lifetime Achievement Award" from the Water Resources Institute, and the "James Krieger Meritorious Service Award" from the Riverside County Bar Association.

His community service record is exceptional in the fields of education, the environment, and civil rights. His leadership in the community has been recognized with top awards from Riverside Community College Foundation, Greater Riverside Chambers of Commerce, Monday Morning Group, City of Riverside, Phi Delta Kappa, the Mission Inn Foundation, and the Riverside Civic League.

Publisher's Acknowledgments

This book was made possible with support from Cal Humanities, a non-profit partner of the National Endowment for the Humanities. Visit www.calhum.org. A Cal Humanities Community Stories fund grant has allowed the Inlandia Institute to publish this memoir. Many thanks to project partners: Riverside Unified School District; University of California, Riverside, Department of History; the Riverside Human Relations Commission; the Martin Luther King, Jr. Visionaries; the African American Historical Society; the Riverside Chapter of the NAACP; the Mexican American Historical Society; and Center for Social Justice and Civil Liberties. We would also like to thank humanities advisor and contributor of the foreward for *No Easy Way*, V.P. Franklin. He is a widely published author and Distinguished Professor of History and Education at the University of California, Riverside, where he holds a University of California President's Chair. He is also editor of *The Journal of African American History*. Thanks also to our community advisor Jack Clarke, Jr., a partner at Best Best & Krieger, a board member of the Riverside County Bar Association, and a winner of the NAACP 2011 Omar Stratton Award. Our gratitude to Terry Bridges, whose support of the fundraising effort ensured the publication of this book. Susan Straight's contribution of her perspective for the Introduction was generous and is highly valued. Dawn Hassett's work as editor and interviewer and Douglas McCulloh's photographs helped bring this book to life. Our special and heartfelt appreciation for all of the community members who gave so generously of their time to be interviewed.

In addition, we would like to recognize and thank the following donors who have helped make this project possible.

INITIATING SPONSORS
Cal Humanities
Best Best and Krieger

LEAD SPONSORS
Inland Empire Chapter of the Federal Bar Association
Walter & Betty Parks
Riverside African American Historical Society
Riverside County Bar Association
Riverside East Rotary
Chuck Wilson & Marion Mitchell-Wilson

SUPPORTING SPONSORS
Kathy & John Allavie
Richard & Lorraine Anderson
Alfred & Betty Bonnett
Terry & Sharon Bridges
In Honor of Larry Burns
William and Ann De Wolfe
Ali & Ellen Estilai

Frank T. & Lucy Heyming
Mike & Karen O'Rourke
Virginia A. Phillips
Barbara & Doug Shackelton
UCR Extension

PARTICIPATING SPONSORS
Connie L. Beasley
Dr. Chuck & Sally Beaty
Jane C. Block
Jill Boulet Murray
Sylvia Broadbent
Carlos & Laurel Cortes
John and Sharon Duffy
Friends of the Riverside Public Library
Mike Gardner
Larry & Gillian Geraty
Shannon Hammock
Tracy Kahn & Norm Ellstrand
Jeff Kraus
Karen Rae & Bruce Kraut

Judy Lee
Ron & Marsha Loveridge
David & Barbara Moore
David Munoz & Victoria Waddle
Helen & Elio Palacios, Jr.
Lloyd B. Porter, Esq.
John & Linda Rhoades
Riverside Historical Society
Rodolfo & Irene Ruibal
Jo & Justin Scott-Coe
Susan Simonin
Ben F. Stoltzfus
Susan Straight
Dave & Sue Struthers
The Why Nots
Lewis J. & Mollie Vanderzyl
John Vineyard & Carole Green
Terry & Cathleen Walling
Carole & Jim Ward
Kathy Wright & Dwight Tate